MW00581976

Instructions for using AR

LET AUGMENTED REALITY CHANGE HOW YOU READ A BOOK

With your smartphone, iPad or tablet you can use the **Hasmark AR** app to invoke the augmented reality experience to literally read outside the book.

  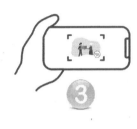

1. Download the **Hasmark app** from the **Apple App Store** or **Google Play**

2. Open and select the (vue) option

3. Point your lens at the full image with the and enjoy the augmented reality experience.

Go ahead and try it right now with the Hasmark Publishing International logo.

MANAGEMENT
IN
BALANCE

ENDORSEMENTS FOR *MICHAEL LERARIO*

Congratulations! You've just been appointed to a managerial position. As the euphoria of selection fades and the uncertainty of your readiness begins to build, relax. Mike Lerario has provided the handbook for you to follow. Mike's management framework provides the core essentials for success in a straightforward, easy to read style. Go with the hard copy – you're going to want to tab, highlight, and keep this book close at hand during your management journey! Already an 'old hand'? I guarantee you'll learn some new things, be reminded of things you've forgotten, and gain clarity on why some of your managerial actions produced less than ideal results...I found myself taking notes.

—**Ken Tovo**,
Lieutenant General, U.S. Army, retired

Fulcrum Centric Leadership is a proven model that Mike continues to expand upon and refine. His theories and methods in Leadership, and *Management in Balance* are proven in both military and business worlds

—**Charles Ritter,**
Sergeant Major, U.S. Army J.F.K.
Special Warfare Center and School

Mike provides another thoughtful book, this one devoted to an examination of the discipline and domains of management, useful to leaders and managers, aspiring managers, and students of management. He writes with clarity and simplicity about a complex and much studied topic. As in his previous book, *Leadership in the Balance*, Mike draws from his considerable experience as an observer and practitioner of leadership and management and provides a practical way to consider the art of management and its essential elements.

—Hank Kinnison,
retired Infantry Colonel and business executive

Compelling. Informative. Mike Lerario's *Management in Balance* delivers a fresh perspective and concise resource for today's managers at all levels of government and business.

—Timothy Kuklo,
Colonel (Retired), MD, JD

Management in Balance is timely, simple and practical. Once again, Mike Lerario has masterfully drilled down to the essentials. Just as he did in his first book *Leadership in Balance*, Mike has identified core domains of management and created an easily understood framework around people, things (Time, Material, Risk and Change) and processes that every new (and even tenured) manager can read today and begin implementing tomorrow! Like one wise man once said: Manage things, Lead people.

—Rob Nielsen,
CEO, All American Leadership

Mike Lerario, and Crispian Consulting, have been an integral part of Hibbett | Gear's Leader Development program for years. In addition to using his books, Mike frequently conducts professional development programs for us, teaches sessions, and conducts executive coaching. I highly recommend you join me and the tens of thousands of other people who believe in its effectiveness. Take it from me, you must make *Leadership in Balance* and *Management in Balance* part of your leadership journey.

—Mike Longo,
CEO, Hibbet Inc.

Mike's keynote address at our Spring Innovation Summit received the highest marks. His insights on leadership, management, and innovation set the tone for our conference and his book *Leadership in Balance* is now the cornerstone for our 'leaders at every level' strategy.

—Patrick Emmons –
Founder, DRAGONSPEARS

As the leader of a large Industrial OEM, I engaged Mike Lerario to provide training to ~300 mechanical contractors and to provide front line leadership training in our manufacturing facility. He tailored the two programs to fit specific business needs and brought in subject matter experts that reinforced key topics. Mike's practical leadership development programs were backed up by years of research and his personal leadership journey (which is inspiring). He didn't bombard audiences with slides and instead took a hands-on approach that resonated with leaders at all levels. Overall, both programs were outstanding investments - relatively low-cost, easy to implement, and high-business impact.

If your business could benefit from improving skilled labor recruiting, engagement, and retention (and quickly) then you should engage Crispian consulting. I will continue to bring them in to every business that I lead going forward.

—Elliot Zimmer,
C-Suite Executive, Industrial Manufacturing

MANAGEMENT
IN
BALANCE

Mike Lerario

TABLE OF CONTENTS

CHAPTER 1

INTRODUCTION

Donna Frazier is a research scientist who, for more than two decades, worked in the medical department of a large medical center conducting research and data analysis. She loved the work and was outstanding at it; Donna was rated the best in her field by her boss and her peers. She found beauty in numbers, and in the hidden and often complex relationships between variables that emerged with analyses and modeling. She often described herself as a "Data Potato."

But as good as Donna was at her job, she felt that she had reached a plateau both in terms of her career and her personal development. She was working at a hospital where the clinical revenue trumped research endeavors. She felt frustrated by the lack of resources available for the research she loved.

So, when she was offered a job with a large pharmaceutical company, she decided to take a leap of faith, changing jobs and work environments. For the first year everything was great. She loved the work, she loved the people she worked with, and she really liked her boss.

Donna immersed herself in her work, and instantly had an impact on process and outcome for her new employer. Once again, she was in a position of being recognized as an expert in her field, a top performer, but it wasn't long before her supervisor started talking with his boss about a new plan for Donna.

Management

Donna wasn't asked, she was told that she would be promoted to management and given responsibility for getting a new drug to market. The drug in question was one that she had been working on for the last 10 months, but now, she would have to manage the entire team as the drug came out of a successful Phase 3 trial. Instead of being primarily focused on data, she would now have the ultimate responsibility and accountability for her team as she leads them in creating the medical narrative, generating additional supporting data, developing, and executing the scientific publication plan for abstracts and manuscripts, and creating educational products. She would also need to manage her team's collaborations with cross-functional partners in marketing, regulatory, and legal to launch the new drug.

To say that she felt scared—totally unprepared and overwhelmed—would be an understatement. She was also afraid to refuse the promotion. Would she be able to keep her current job if she didn't accept the promotion? Wouldn't it be a red flag on her resume to have left a job after less than a year? Donna felt backed into a corner with no options. What seemed like her dream job last week was turning into a total nightmare with the decision to move her to "management."

How does this happen?

As is often the case with outstanding employees, senior leadership takes notice of them and considers them likely candidates for management positions within the company. And why not? As we know from Jim Collins' work, great organizations promote from within.

The problem, generally, is that senior leadership makes these decisions, and personnel moves with little to no regard for:

1. The desires of the person involved; they assume that everyone wants a "promotion."
2. The difference between performance and potential.
3. The training and development needed to shift from "individual contributor" to "management/leadership."

This happens not because the senior leadership is evil or stupid, although that is a remote possibility. It happens because they are in a hurry: in a hurry to fill an important position; in a hurry to accomplish this quarter's sales, revenue, and profit targets; and in a hurry to move on. They don't spend time or money developing people like Donna because that's an expense without an obvious immediate return on investment. And besides, Donna is good at her job, so she'll figure this out...

Inevitably, the company sees one of three outcomes:

1. Donna and her team fail.
2. Donna and her team struggle but eventually figure it out.
3. Donna is a "natural" and excels in this new management role.

It may take some time before both the company and Donna learn which of these scenarios is their new operational reality. However, one thing they can count on right away is that a promotion to management that is based solely on performance as an individual contributor guarantees you will have lost your best performer.

When I say that a company will lose its best performer, I'm not talking about that person leaving the company, although that may happen eventually. When you promote your best performer to a management position, be they an analyst, welder, salesperson, computer programmer, you name it, you have lost them in the position where they excel. Instead, you have placed them into a role they may not be prepared for and may not have any interest in doing.

Two out of the three outcomes listed above are suboptimal in the immediate term, and even the third outcome might take some time to see the desired results. And in my experience, the first outcome is not only unacceptable, but also unnecessary and avoidable.

We see this across all types of business and in every kind of organization. Promotions should always be based on performance and merit; however, a shift from "production" to "management" requires more consideration of Donna's leadership and management potential, as well as her interest in the change.

How then to avoid this situation where two out of three likely outcomes involve dysfunction and reduced performance by the team and the manager, and all three involve the loss of your best performer?

Whether you are senior leadership or an individual contributor, the way out and the way ahead is to be more aware of what you want and more invested in your people's and/or your own development.

Senior leadership must ask themselves some important questions when considering personnel changes: What skills and attributes do they have now, and which skills and attributes can they develop over time? What is the individual's interest in or desire for moving to a leadership/management track? Where is the individual best suited to work and can we afford to keep them in that role? If a move is required for the good of the company, how do we prepare the individual for that move?

Individuals like Donna must be aware of what the options are within an organization. They must know what it really means to be a manager—not just the difference in pay, but the differences in respon-sibility and workload. They must know and consider the tradeoffs, as well as what they will leave behind and what they will gain.

Donna must also take responsibility for her own training and development. If she desires a management position, she must seek out training and development opportunities. This is no different if she wants to remain an individual contributor. Keeping current on best practices and techniques are keys to individual performance, but it's the habit of learning how to learn and how to grow that matters most.

Success and failure in any organization hinge on getting this right.

In a world where most of us see things as a question of "either/or," I've come to realize that success is more often about "both/and." The best options, choices, and solutions are almost always a matter of balance and finding the equilibrium between opposites or opposing ideas. Choosing between one or the other is a false dichotomy and can have destructive results. Recognizing our ability to find the equilibrium between opposites allows us to find a better and more balanced approach to life and work.

It's not a question of either awareness or development, success requires both/and. It's not a question of the individual actions of senior leaders or individual contributors, as both have a role in achieving a success-ful outcome.

I wrote my first book, *Leadership in Balance*, to help people like Donna understand the essence of leadership and how to find balance between how they naturally wanted to lead and what the situation demanded of them. I offer it as a model and a plan for the new, emerging, and high-potential leader that never had any formal training, or to supple-ment any training they might have received. *Leadership in Balance* is a specific view of leadership and a companion to this book. They are similar with regard to structure, but they are different because leadership and management are different.

The difference between management and leadership—and how, when, and why to find the balance between the two—is a subject for another day. It's also the subject of my next book, but for now, we need to define management in terms of the essential domains and the conditions that frame them.

What follows here is more than just a "how to" lesson on management. It's a model for finding efficiencies in the things we manage. It's a way to accomplish your mission and the tasks assigned to you and your team, but also a way to build a better and stronger team. Your first job is always what the position description says, but your "second" job is to develop the people you oversee.

No one should have to face the choices that Donna found herself with and senior leaders can do better in making sure they build a great team by assessing not just performance, but potential and desire. Until that happens, the pages that follow offer a way for Donna and folks like her, plucked from the ranks and doing great work, to become more natural in how they manage and to find the way to success in their new role.

CHAPTER 2

DOMAINS OF MANAGEMENT
AND THEIR CONDITIONS

I f you are reading this book, you might be like Donna, who did not necessarily seek out her new management position. Alternatively, you may have desired a management position without fully understanding how that was different from your work as an individual contributor, and you may find yourself lost in terms of how to prepare yourself for that role. It could be that you have observed a similar scenario at work. Perhaps you were the senior leader who promoted someone into a management position because they were great at their job, and you needed to fill that position right away. But the person struggled in the new position, and now you realize that talent alone is never enough.

Regardless of your role or path to a management position, you quickly see that management is not the simple equation of your job as an individual contributor multiplied by the number of people you supervise. Management is much more than just the collective efforts of everyone on your team.

Throughout my life, I have had the opportunity to lead and to manage, and I have formally studied both subjects. I have a master's degree in leadership development and hold professional certifications in project management.

I wrote *Leadership in Balance*, in part, to share my thoughts and views on arguably one of the most researched and chronicled aspects of human interaction: leadership. Because my primary audience for that work is the new or the emergent leader, I distilled leadership down to its most essential elements. I concluded that these elements are Communication, Adaptability, Focus, and Influence.

Leadership is a very personal discipline, and people often refer to their "leadership style." Therefore, I frame the four essential leadership domains by their opposite tendencies. The *exclusive* tendency, when taken to the extreme, excludes everything and everyone else in its environment. Its opposite is the *inclusive* tendency, which draws all influences from everyone and everything else in the environment.

Using my Leadership Fulcrum Assessment™, leaders come to understand their natural tendency in all four domains, but they must also become aware of the situation where they lead and what that demands of them. Finally, whenever the situation demands something other than their natural tendency, they must learn to "Be the Fulcrum"®. Taken together, these three steps are what constitutes my Fulcrum-Centric Leadership® model.

Over the last few years, I've had the opportunity to address a wide array of audiences on a variety of leadership topics. However, more and more frequently I'm asked to speak about how "management" and "leadership" are distinct disciplines. In fact, it was a keynote address I gave in Memphis, Tennessee in the fall of 2021 that inspired me to write a book that outlines and defines those differences.

But that's not the subject of this book. That will be my third book: *Solving the Leaders Dilemma!*

This book sets out to define management as a discipline separate from leadership, and will answer the questions: "What are the four essential domains of management?" and "What does it mean to manage with balance?"

So, what is management and how should we define it?

I believe the four essential domains of management are Time, Material, Risk, and Change. That's it. If you can look at the environment and its conditions for each domain, you can manage most effectively for the current state AND for any future states. Of course, there are other aspects of management that might be called a domain (cost management comes to mind), but these other aspects are all influenced and impacted by how we manage Time, Material, Risk, and Change.

And similar to how the domains of leadership are defined by their opposite tendencies, the essential management domains are defined by the extreme conditions that anchor them.

Notice that I said "extreme conditions," not tendencies. That's because management is not personal in the way that leadership is personal. I don't believe that we have a natural tendency for management domains, but we do prefer what we are most comfortable with. In the real world, across all four of the management domains, we will find a condition that lies someplace between abundance and scarcity. At first glance, we might be tempted to assign a value judgement to each extreme, but either could be a positive or a negative depending on one's management of that condition.

Time

I define the management domain of "Time" as "deliberate" with extreme abundance and "dynamic" with extreme scarcity. Let me outline what I mean with each, and then we will explore the positive and negative outcomes they might generate.

With an abundance of time, we can be very deliberate in how we plan and how we manage tasks. That means that we can explore more options and examine the potential outcomes of various choices. With scarce amounts of time, our choices become more constrained, and we must be dynamic in how we plan and how we execute.

The upside to being deliberate is the detail and the attention we can give to everything we do. It provides us the time (and space) to think about more, to examine more, and to try more. On the downside, the most obvious problem with having an abundance of time is the tendency to lose sight of our objective, or to even procrastinate and miss deadlines.

This contrasts with a scarcity of time, where missing a deadline or doing a poor job is all too often the result of too much to do and not enough time to do it. That's the downside of dynamic, but the upside to not having a lot of time is that it forces us to prioritize and adapt and make choices.

Material

The "Material" domain is defined as "wasteful" with extreme abundance and as "wanting" with extreme scarcity. The term "wasteful" generally holds a negative connotation but the word "abundance" is generally seen as a positive thing, so how can an abundance of materials be bad? Again, we are framing the extreme cases, and without question, an abundance of materials makes life easier. We can manage time better when we have all the materials needed to build or produce our products. But at the same time, an abundance of material can naturally lead to wasteful actions and a careless regard for the value of things. Thus, the downside is that in this condition we set ourselves up for failure should we have a future need for materials that we previously treated so carelessly. We only need to look at supply chain disruptions in the wake of the COVID 19 pandemic to see how quickly, and without warning, we can move from abundance to scarcity.

On the other end of the spectrum of material management, we have the condition of "wanting." A lack of supplies, tools, or other material things means we risk mission accomplishment or even the existence of our job. If we cannot produce because of insufficient materials, that is a real threat to our existence as an organization or a company. However, if we develop an appreciation of wanting, we can see the opportunity to be creative, proactive (to get ahead of the supply chain), and inventive. It might drive us to other sources, other materials, or even other markets. This is can also drive our ability to diversify as resources and markets shift.

Risk

We define the "Risk" domain between "fearful" when there is abundance and "reckless" when there is scarcity. With both Time and Material, the natural reaction is to look at "abundance" as better than "scarcity." With Risk and Change, that reaction is flipped, and scarcity starts looking like the positive and abundance looks like the negative condition.

With an abundance of risk, we may become fearful. We may slow down, or even back away from the task to be managed. That fear can affect our judgement and our ability to make decisions as the "fight, flight, or freeze" function of our animal brains kicks in. As natural as those reactions to risk are, deep down inside we recognize that the greatest rewards are connected to the greatest risks. Learning how to manage risk is not just a way to keep the organization safe, it is absolutely the path to the greatest outcomes.

With a scarcity of risk, the extreme condition is to become reckless. If we see little to no risk, or if we don't understand the risks involved, we can become carefree and rash in our decisions and what we are willing to do. Over time, we might forget how to do an assessment of risk and that can spill over into other parts of our life, and certainly into other tasks at work. Therefore, risk must always be calculated so that we know what is acceptable and what is not.

Change

When there is an abundance of change, the extreme condition is "volatility" and when there is a scarcity of change, we call that "fossilization."

Volatility is defined as "rapid and unpredictable change," and it can generate problems for the other three domains of management as well as drive up costs. But on a positive note, if you can manage change in a volatile condition, your abilities in all other areas will be sharpened and strengthened in the process.

Contrast that with the condition of scarcity in the domain of change. If nothing ever changes, management becomes easy and thoughtless in a way that can make us comfortable. So comfortable in fact, that like a dinosaur bone frozen in time, we become a fossil. Sooner or later, change will come to us and our organization; but if fossilization has taken hold, we will not be able to change, and like the dinosaurs, we will also become extinct.

In all four domains, especially Change Management, managers must understand the nature of the current condition and consider that against what they believe the future holds. Failure to do this has been the downfall of many companies that couldn't respond to disruptive innovation. [1]

Over the course of the next few chapters, I will expound on the definitions of these four management domains. I will also provide you with

---

[1] The term "disruptive innovation" was developed by Clayton Christensen to describe how some companies can deal with change while others fail, which he writes about in his book *The Innovator's Dilemma*. Another good source for seeing the need for balance in what we currently do (or can do) as a company versus what the future holds is *Lead and Disrupt* by Charles A. O'Reilly and Michael Tushman

examples where the contrast between "abundant" and "scarce" conditions is most clearly visible.

What about balance? As we move forward, I will work to show you how you can achieve balance in each of these essential domains. Balance between what you are comfortable doing against the condition that exists, but also balance between your current condition in that domain and the condition that you will likely encounter in your future.

My hope is that by the time we are through, you will see the value in equilibrium and your role as manager to achieve it regardless of the conditions where you must manage.

CHAPTER 3

TIME MANAGEMENT

"What is important is seldom urgent, and what is urgent is seldom important."

— Dwight D. Eisenhower

Time Defined

"Time is the continued sequence of existence and events that occurs in an apparently irreversible succession from the past, through the present, into the future. It is a component quantity of various measurements used to sequence events, to compare the duration of events or the intervals between them, and to quantify rates of change of quantities in material reality or in the conscious experience. Time is often referred to as a fourth dimension, along with three spatial dimensions."[2]

This definition from Wikipedia goes beyond our examination of time as a management domain, in that we will not ponder its "apparently irreversible" nature. Assuming that time is finite and unretrievable once it passes, the essence of time as a management domain rests in

---

[2] Wikipedia https://en.wikipedia.org/wiki/Time

the middle part of this definition: a measure to sequence events, compare durations and intervals, and ultimately, make decisions on how time will be spent or utilized.

Time, therefore, should be viewed as both a measurement device and a resource. That said, it is such an important resource that it gets its own domain; we'll discuss all other resources (excluding people) in the next chapter, Material Management.

The fleeting nature of time demands respect, and it can also engender fear. Most other resources left unused can be employed at some later date. This is not the case with time. Unused time still passes, and that is why the management of time is so important.

Another element to consider is that time can be both relative or absolute in its measure, and this affects whether we have an abundance or a scarcity of it. A difficult task with a relatively long amount of time allotted to it is not the same as an easy task with the same time to complete. As an example, in relative terms, twelve months seems like an abundance of time, especially if the task is simple—such as developing a new process for inspecting lumber yards. However, for a difficult task like developing, testing, and delivering a new vaccine, twelve months is in the scarcity condition.

Abundance

The abundance condition for Time Management is "Deliberate." I use this term because, with an abundance of time, we can be very deliberate about everything we do. We can "take our time" and consider every imaginable option and outcome before and during each task.

In general, and for most people, an abundance of time is not only a luxury, but also the condition they hope for. Who wouldn't want more time in any and every aspect of their life? Being deliberate and taking things slowly has great benefits; we can train our people, we can do more in and for our communities, and we can make changes as needs be. However, there are drawbacks and potential pitfalls to this "deliberate" condition of time management.

First, it is critical to recognize that too much time can be as difficult to manage as too little time. While the abundance condition seems like it would be of greater benefit, it is often the cause of poor outcomes when the manager or the team procrastinates. Having a lot of time and being deliberate can lull one into a false sense of security. This becomes even more impactful if we are suddenly faced with problems or changes that we did not anticipate or even consider.

Scarcity

Most managers, especially new managers, look at this condition with some level of anxiety. They wonder how they and their team could ever manage to complete all their tasks. They wonder how that failure will impact the team and the larger organization. Importantly, they are concerned for their reputation and the prospects for future growth and promotions. In general, they only see the negatives of having a scarcity of time.

There is, however, opportunity with this condition. A scarcity of time can force you to be more inventive and creative. It can help you prioritize, and to limit the things you and your team try to do. Less time can drive efficiencies in your process and programs.

Which condition are you in and what is the status?

Your first job as manager is to understand what condition you are currently in, and whether that condition is permanent or temporary. This understanding is essential for your ability to operate in the current moment and prepare for the future state.

Signs of time abundance include not being rushed or pressed to accomplish tasks, finishing "early," and always having time to do more.

Time scarcity includes the opposite of these things and leaves you with a sense of dread for the task, not just for the passing of time.

Because time is relative to the difficulty or complexity of the tasks, you must assess each task for any dependencies or connections that will affect task completion. This includes things you need other people or other teams to do before you can start or finish your tasks. Often these dependencies and relations are much easier to identify than a shift in available time, so look for them first.

To find equilibrium with time management, you must use the "excess" time afforded you when you have an abundance of time. Pull your team together to create processes and procedures that make routine as many aspects of the job as possible. The purpose of this, and the outcome you need, is to remove decisions from day-to-day operations wherever and whenever that is possible. If you can eliminate the need to make decisions, you will automatically save time and your team will find freedom in the routine. Let me say that again: your team will find freedom in the routine. Not having to make decisions on the things that are routine and happen the same way all the time, frees you and them to think and act on the important, and possibly urgent, things that are outside of routine. Their ability to move and act quickly will greatly improve and you will set them up for scarcity when the condition for time management shifts or changes.

If you are already in the scarcity condition, you will find equilibrium by keeping your team on task. You will have to manage the relationships between teams and the relationship between processes to ensure your team has every bit of available time allotted to the important aspects of your tasks. This requires you to be proactive in making sure that your team isn't waiting on someone else to finish their task if there is dependency between what you are doing and what they are doing. You may not be able to influence what the other teams are doing, but with a better picture of how those other teams are doing, you can adjust tasks and timing within your team to get ahead of delays or accelerated timelines.

General Concepts for Time Management

We can waste time by doing nothing or by doing things that don't facilitate accomplishing our assigned tasks. We cannot create more time, but we can manage the tasks we take on, essentially creating time by subtraction, not addition. Therefore, time management is essentially task management. Establishing priorities allows us to decide which activities and tasks will get our attention and is the best way to manage time. You, as the manager, will establish the priorities for your team or hold them accountable to the priority set by the boss. Therefore, it's essential that your entire team and anyone that interacts with them fully understands what that priority is.

1. Mission Statements

Mission statements are an expression of task and purpose, and every organization should have a clear understanding of their "mission." Stated another way, an organization must know *what* it is they do, and more importantly, *why* they are doing it.

Absent this statement of task and purpose, your organization will likely wander from project to project, avoiding the most essential tasks for no other reason than the other tasks were easier or seemed more interesting.

Begin by listing all the tasks you have been given or assigned. Next, identify the most important tasks within that list; your essential tasks are the ones that if you didn't complete successfully, you would fail the overall mission of your team.

Now identify your purpose—the reason you are doing these tasks. Is it for profit? Is it for making the world a better place? Why does any of this matter? The answers to these questions are the beacon to guide you when you lack clear direction to move. You and your team can apply this mission statement to focus amid distractions and to guide their initiative.

A clear understanding of what must be done to succeed (key tasks), and why those things matter and are worth doing (purpose), is the best way for you to manage time and tasks with your team.

2. Eisenhower Decision Matrix

Dwight D. Eisenhower, Supreme Allied Commander in Europe during World War II and the 34th President of the United States, is quoted as saying: "What is important is seldom urgent, and what is urgent is seldom important."

Stephen Covey used that quotation in his book *The 7 Habits of Highly Effective People* to create a two-by-two matrix using the ideas of urgent and important, which he coined The Eisenhower Decision Matrix.

The top left quadrant shows tasks that are both urgent and important. These are the tasks that you (or your team) must do well. Because they are urgent, they must be done now. So long as we can truly know what is important and what is urgent, tasks in this quadrant should be the exception and not the rule. Crises and emergencies, including emergencies that are "man-made" because someone screwed up or left things to the last minute, are the types of things we're talking about here. That said, I'm reminded of the saying, "Poor planning on your part doesn't constitute an emergency on my part." In other words, don't get pulled into someone else's drama; this quadrant is for things that are important and urgent for *you or your team*. This includes what is urgent and important for your boss, your owners, and your customers. An inability to understand this will cause you to spend way more time doing things that seem urgent but aren't important, or things that seem important but could wait.

The top right quadrant is for tasks that are important but not urgent. Tasks that fall into this quadrant require more of our efforts and energy, but because they are not urgent, we are prone to forget about them or to keep putting them off since it seems we have a lot of time. Left too long, you will find that tasks that started in this quadrant will suddenly appear in the top left quadrant, and you'll have to drop other things to accomplish them. These could be anything from planning for your retirement to working on your secession plan, or the development of the people on your team. My experience is that it's best to carve out a bit of time daily or weekly to work on these tasks, or to at least check in on them routinely until they are done.

The bottom left quadrant is for the tasks that are urgent but not important. It's identified as the delegation quadrant for a reason: it's the best place to train your people. A task that isn't important is low risk for delegation and could be a great learning opportunity for someone on your team. And if it is urgent, the pressure to get it done will add to the learning experience for the person doing it. Tasks in this quadrant include meetings and calls that don't require a decision, or briefings to provide information to outside agencies. When you delegate in this quadrant, you need to carve out time to conduct a review with the person you sent in your place to make the most of this as a learning and growth opportunity for them.

The final quadrant, in the bottom right, is for tasks that are not urgent and not important. I used to call this the "my sons are playing video games" quadrant, and while I agree that we shouldn't do work tasks in this quadrant, it's a different story in our personal lives. Not urgent and not important could apply to many things that we do to decompress and relax. That's not to diminish the value of taking time off and relaxing to avoid burnout; in that regard, tasks in this quadrant serve a purpose. The key is to minimize the time you spend in this quadrant so you can spend more time, attention, and energy on those things that are important.

Tools, Techniques, and Tips for Time Management

Here is where the technical aspects of management come into play. The following tools and tips can help you manage time and tasks within your team. There are books and courses dedicated to each, and I have provided resources at the end of the book if you wish to dig deeper.

1. Gantt Charts

First developed in the late nineteenth century by Polish engineer Karol Adamiecki, Gantt Charts were made popular in the early twentieth century by Henry Gantt, a management consultant and engineer. Simply stated, Gantt Charts are a visual representation of tasks and events performed over time. All activities are shown as bars with start and end dates so that the longer the task, the longer the bar. The Gantt Chart also allows you to see which tasks are being done simultaneously or sequentially.

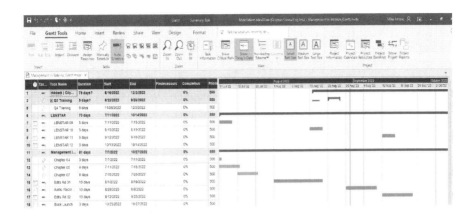

Gantt Charts can be made by hand, by using a spreadsheet, or by using specialized software.[3] Pictured above is a Gantt Chart I created using the MindView 8.0 software to map out the final steps of writing this book, but also to track the significant client work I needed to accomplish at the same time.

The general format is to list all the actions, activities, and events down the left side of the chart with the timeline of the project across the top. The timeline can be in any incremental amount (usually days, weeks, and months), but it must begin with the start date for all activities and end with the scheduled date for conclusion.

Each task or action has its own line and often includes additional information such as name, task owner, total duration, start date, and end date. The task is represented using a bar to graphicly display the start date and end date under the timeline. Once all tasks are displayed, you can easily see when tasks are happening at the same time, and/or the sequencing of each task. This allows you to understand in one look where your busiest and most resource-dependent periods will be.

---

[3] You can learn more about Gantt Charts and find software solutions at https://www. gantt.com/

If you have an abundance of time, the Gantt Chart allows you to see where you can delay the start of any task to relieve some of the overlap or intensity of the project and the people working it. Similarly, when time is scarce, the chart allows you to see how your tasks are distributed, and this may allow you to advance actions in the timeline to ensure everything gets accomplished on time.

2. PERT Diagrams and Critical Path Method (CPM)

PERT is an acronym for Program Evaluation and Review Technique. It was developed by the United States Navy in the 1950s. PERT allows you to see the minimum amount of time required to complete a task and is better to use when you want to know how the steps in a task or project affect each other. Dependencies are identified and this allows you to understand where there is "slack" to delay steps without impacting any other part of the project.

Events and milestones (nodes) are represented as boxes or numbers on the PERT diagram, and arrows connecting the nodes represent sequence and which events can be done at the same time.

PERT also identifies the "critical path" which is the longest activity to accomplish and doesn't have slack to delay without "crashing" it.

Like PERT, Critical Path Management (CPM) was developed by project management experts working with businesses for essentially the same reasons: management of the time and tasks of complex projects. Central to both methods is defining the "critical" path and the relationships and dependencies between activities and events.

As we discussed earlier, time is relative to task complexity and difficulty. PERT and CPM were developed to manage the timelines of complex tasks, so these two techniques lend themselves to the condition of scarcity.

Neither method is particularly difficult to learn, and whole books, articles, and training programs are available for any manager who wants to learn more.[4]

3. Alternatives to "Yes"

One of the biggest demands on our time and energy is doing a task for someone else. While it can be rewarding to do things for other people, it comes at an opportunity cost: other things that we can do with our time and energy. This effect is magnified when you consider that the things you say "yes" to impact everyone that you are trying to help and everyone waiting on you to get back to your assigned tasks. Remember, when you say "yes" to one thing, you are saying "no" to something else you might do instead.

This can be particularly draining when the "ask" is coming from someone who probably has (or should have) the time and resources to do it themselves. If the request is coming from one of your teammates, the "ask" becomes a missed opportunity for their growth and development if you take it on and do the work for them.

What can you do then when someone asks you to spend time and energy on something when you don't want to, or when you think it's best for their development if they do it themselves? Here are a few suggestions:

- Gain time and space. Instead of immediately answering "Yes," respond with "Let me think about it." This gives you time to consider your options, but it also gives them time to reconsider the "ask" and think about what they can/should do. This is equally important when your boss asks you (versus tells you) to do or

---

[4] PERT and CPM have numerous online resources, but this article from the Harvard Business Review does a great job of explaining CPM https://hbr.org/1963/09/the-abcs-of-the-critical-path-method

consider something. This can be a more delicate situation, and you must be tactful and get back to them as soon as possible with your thoughts and options. With peers or people who work for you, it's more about being respectful than tactful, and it can be a great learning point as you work through the options with them once you both have had time and space to think about it.

- Tell them "No" and offer an alternative. If you respond to the request with "No, but here's what I can do…" you are negotiating for your time and energy. This allows you to set the conditions and still help in a way that works for you.

- Tell them "Yes" with conditions, such as requiring their participation. "Yes, I can do that and here's what I'm going to need from you." This approach requires them to commit to the project/task as well. In the end, you may find that they are not that invested and the whole thing goes away.

While all the above alternatives are best used with peers and teammates, you might find yourself being asked to do more by your boss. And while you generally should not tell your boss "No," she or he must know the cost of you taking on an additional task or project. Explain to them that while you can do this new or additional thing, it comes at a cost to some other task or project. Explain the potential impacts and recommend a prioritization of tasks if you find yourself in this position.

Your time, effort, and energy are your most valuable resources. You must do what you need to do for you and what you committed to do for others. Saying "yes" all the time or too often will burn you out, cause you to regret your choices, and resent the person who asked for your help.

4. To-do Lists

Most of us have so many things competing for our time and attention, that we can benefit from building a daily task list. I recommend doing this either first thing in the morning for that day, or at the end of the day for the things you must do tomorrow. As you list your tasks, a good technique to make sure you are doing the important stuff first is to categorize every task by its importance, assigning it a number: 1, 2, or 3.

1 = Something you must get done that day.

This is the important task(s) for that day. Depending on what they are, there probably shouldn't be more than three tasks with a number **1** next to them.

2 = Something that would be nice to get done that day.

It's not urgent, but if you have time, you should do it that day.

3 = Something that can wait until tomorrow.

Wait until tomorrow? Why would I include this on my task list? It's on your list because you want to visualize other things coming up, and things with the number **3** next to them might be ideal tasks to delegate to someone else. This is a great way to get these things done and develop your people at the same time.

5. Batching Time

There are probably things you want to accomplish and manage that are routine. We might call them the "big rocks," and like the analogy of filling a container with different sized rocks and sand, you will never get them all into the container if you don't start with the biggest things first.

As an example, with all the tasks I must do in a day as I run my business and try to write books, writing is a big rock: it helps me to think more clearly about everything, and it helps define who I am as both a trainer and a coach. That said, if I don't set aside the time to write, I can quickly be overcome by events and start doing other smaller (easier) things instead.

My solution to this is to set aside two hours every morning to write. This batching of time helps me stay on track both in terms of my writing and for the rest of my day. Batching it for the same time each and every day helps me stay accountable to the important tasks, and this routine frees up time throughout the day for other tasks.

I do this for other parts of my professional life and for my personal life. I try to do all my coaching calls on Fridays, batching them by the day and hour. I set aside time to call my parents every Sunday, a practice begun when I went back to Afghanistan in 2013 after eight years away from that war.

Decide what your most important tasks are and if they are routine or work best with a set schedule; block off the hours, days, or even weeks to attend to them. You'll find that your time management and task accomplishment will both improve. Batching your meetings is another area you might want to consider going forward as well. Establishing a routine such as having recurring meetings on the same day/time or batching half a day each week for necessary meetings are examples.

6. Meeting Management

Meetings consume way too much of our time, and this is true in an office environment whether it be in-person, remote, or hybrid. This is also a concern in factory settings where meetings can pull supervisors off the line when their leadership is most needed.

Learn to successfully manage your meetings and meeting schedules, and you will free up massive amounts of time and increase productivity.

The first and most important step in meeting management is to purge the schedule of unnecessary meetings. What's an unnecessary meeting? Simply, it is any meeting where the objective can be accomplished with an email or a phone call. This will likely eliminate 40-80 percent of them.

Secondly, limit participants to only the people who must be there. This requires communication with the rest of the team, so a published agenda and complete meeting minutes are essential components of meeting management.

Agendas must be exact and available before the meeting starts. Participants should have input, but once the meeting facilitator decides on the agenda items, you must stick to it. If your company allows it, ensure that the meeting is recorded (video if available) and the transcript is available to all members of the team who need to access the information and outputs of the meeting to do their work effectively. For legal or proprietary reasons, you will likely need to secure the video and any written transcripts. The meeting minutes must include a task list: what is to be done by whom following the meeting.

Meetings must also be for a set time. I find that thirty minutes is often enough, and sixty minutes is probably the maximum time needed for most meetings. You might also benefit from scheduling an occasional fifteen to twenty-minute meeting to update your team on an important project. These are easy to drop if not absolutely necessary, and they are much better than an inbox of unclear emails. If more than one hour is needed, you are probably in need of a workshop, not a meeting. If you cannot get all the agenda items covered in the assigned time, you need to be more aggressive in setting (limiting) the agenda and the discussion.

If you have an abundance of time, you might not be aware of how much time you are spending—and wasting—in meetings. If time is scarce, you are dreading all meetings and your attention will be else-where, making the meetings even less effective.

It may take a change in your organization's culture, but the tips above on meeting management might be the biggest and easiest thing you can do to better manage your time.

7. Take Notes

Taking notes seems to be a lost art, yet one of the first lessons I learned as a cadet at the United States Military Academy is that a professional ALWAYS has something to write with and to write on. As an officer, I always had note cards and a pen in my pocket.

For many years, I carried a "Day Timer" calendar with phone num-bers, contact information, my schedule, and my task list in a pocket-sized booklet. So much of my life was carried in that booklet, I wrote in large print "Reward offered if found" on the inside front page.

I also used a "green notebook" for more detailed notes and tasks. An item from the Federal Supply Service, the green notebook has become ubiquitous among Army Officers and Non-Commissioned Officers. They are so common that it has become used in the name of one of the best military-themed blogs and podcasts.[5]

With my green notebook, I used the right-hand pages to list tasks and projects that I was assigned, or that I assigned to one of my people. Each task started with a box. Once the task was started, I drew a diago-nal line (/) through the box so that I could see it was begun with a simple glance at my list. Once the task was completed, I drew a second diagonal line (\), filling in the box with an "x" to indicate the task was complete. This was an easy way to keep track of all the things I was

---

[5] "From the Green Notebook" is a great reference for critical thinking and reflection. You can find out more at https://fromthegreennotebook.com/

responsible to do, and to be able to see the status of each task in a very general but highly visual way.

Another advantage to carrying this notebook was the space it gave me to write. On the left-hand pages, I wrote my personal thoughts about things I had seen or heard during the day. These later became things for me to remember or to act on as I attained more rank and responsibility. These journal entries gave historical context to the tasks I had and the tasks I assigned to others, and allowed me, in my opinion, to be a better leader whenever I got the chance.

At this point you might think that carrying a notebook or note card is too "old school." You have your smartphone that you can use to take notes, link items to your calendar, and do research at the same time. All true, but here is something I think you should consider: it's not always appropriate to use your phone.

In an industrial setting, it's possible you are not even allowed to have your phone with you for safety reasons. Clearly, our modern phones can be a distraction to our work, and they can also be a security hazard if anyone hacked your phone or activated your camera or microphone to listen in on confidential company discussions. Trust me, this capability exists, and while you think you are not important enough to be the target of such things, you could become the gateway to someone who is.

These two reasons (safety and security) are sufficient for me to recommend the use of note-taking material (i.e., pen and paper). Pen and paper can provide a greater amount of each when used properly, but it also provides you with the opportunity to set an example.

When your phone is in your hand, you could be doing any number of things unrelated to work like social media, texting, emails, etc. When you have a notebook and a pen, it's likely that you are doing only one thing: taking notes.

The bottom line is it doesn't matter what you use if you can do it safely and securely, but you need to have a way to take notes and to keep track of your tasks. People will notice and they will appreciate your ability to stay on task or to help them stay on task, and in so doing, manage time better.

Summary

Time management is really task management. Understanding the difference between things that are urgent and things that are important is your first step. The world of project management provides excellent tools like Gantt Charts, PERT, and CPM. Additionally, to-do lists and meeting management do not require much training, and your productivity and time/task management will improve if you stick with them. Regardless of your time management condition, these tools, tips, and techniques will allow you to be more effective and more efficient.

CHAPTER 4

MATERIAL MANAGEMENT

"Under-resourcing people builds resilience. The most innovative people I know are poor."

— Kevin Owens, Master Sergeant (Ret)

Material Defined

The term "material management" is most often associated with manufacturing where the supply chain and raw materials are essential to production. For our purposes, we'll extend the domain to include any hardware or assets used in any business or within any organization.

As defined by the nonprofit Construction Industry Institute, material management is "the planning and controlling of all material and equipment so they are requested in advance, obtained at a reasonable cost and are available when needed." This definition includes not only materials that go directly into the product and the equipment to produce it, but also the spare parts needed for maintenance, to ensure uninterrupted operations.[6]

---

[6] This section was extracted from the Hexagon website https://hexagonxalt.com/resource-library/what-is-materials-management

Basically, any resource needed to accomplish your work, excluding people and time, can be considered "material" that you must manage.

Abundance

The abundance condition of material management is "Waste." When blessed with an abundance of things, human nature is to value them less. That leads to waste and a misuse of resources. This is the management manifestation of the phrase: "That which we achieve too easily, we esteem too lightly."

Again, this is the extreme condition, and the role of the manager is to prevent movement to the extreme. If you find yourself with unlimited resources, you don't need to worry about getting things done today; instead, worry about what resources you'll have for tomorrow. Having everything we need right now tends to lead us away from thoughts of conservation, efficiency, savings, and planning for scarcity because we are comfortable.

Scarcity

A scarcity of material can drive an organization into bankruptcy, but it can also force an organization to economize, prioritize, and innovate. There is certainly a tipping point beyond which a business cannot function, but if we don't have a lot of resources, we learn to do what we can with what we have. This condition drives us to want more resources, but it can also drive us to be more inventive. A hunger for more is one of the greatest motivators for innovation. For this reason, the condition of scarcity in material management is "Wanting."

Which condition are you in and what is the status?

As a manager, you either have all you need (and perhaps more), or you don't have enough. In the first scenario, the abundance of resources makes it easy for you to do your job and to not worry about supplies, deliveries, tools, fixtures, or raw materials. In the second scenario, when you don't have enough, a shortage of material forces you to make hard choices regarding tasks, production, sales, and deliverables. However, conditions are rarely permanent, and the job of the manager is to deal with the abundance or scarcity of material she or he has now and to prepare for the opposite condition that will likely define the future.

When you have all the material you need, everything seems to go as planned, but it breeds a sense of complacency and comfort. For as long as it lasts, you and your team will not have to do much other than the "plan." If the manager doesn't explicitly address the inevitable change in resource availability through training or other exercises, the team will forget how to function with less-than-optimal resources.

When materials are scarce, production, quality, and sales all suffer. The lack of material slows us down, and upsets our customers, employees, and owners. However, scarcity also drives innovation and efficiencies that we might not otherwise consider. When we carry the lessons of scarcity with us into times of abundance, we become better stewards of all material and more efficient in producing, delivering, and selling. Absent the "wanting," we certainly would drift to wasteful behaviors when things were once again abundant.

General Concepts for Material Management

This domain of management is probably the easiest to understand in terms of our current conditions. The concepts of abundance and scarcity in material management can be addressed as binary, i.e., you have all you need, or you don't have enough. However, the real world is rarely binary. Therefore, a better approach is to consider minimums and optimums. In other words: What is the smallest amount I need and what is the best amount I can use? Below the minimum is failure. Above the optimum is excess; things that we might be able to set aside for future use if we don't "use" them now (to avoid waste).

For this reason, as a manager, you not only need to understand the minimum amount of material needed to be successful, but also the optimum amount of material to reach your fullest possibilities.

As a young paratrooper platoon leader, whenever we had an airborne operation, we would rehearse the plan of attack that was to be implemented once we landed and assembled on the drop zone. The hardest part was the assembly--being dropped from 500 feet or more above ground level, at night, with crosswinds and sometimes in the rain, and occasionally on the wrong drop zone (thanks to the Air Force...)— assembling a group of paratroopers is not easy. It can take all night or even days to get 100% accountability of every trooper who exited the airplane.

So, in rehearsal and in practice, we would establish what percent of the unit we would wait for before moving out to our objective. It might be 40 percent, 50 percent, or some other percentage of the unit. The problem was that different members of the unit were equipped with different weapons and other necessary items. For example, when your mission is to block a major intersection and to stop an armored force from overrunning the drop zone, and the success or failure of the entire operation rests on completing that task, do you wait for all your paratroopers to assemble before moving out to your objective? No, you can't wait. Do you move out with 50 percent, even if all those present are riflemen? No, this would not be smart since you're going up against tanks or some other armored vehicle and rifles alone will not stop them.

The answer and the key to success is understanding what minimum force you need to accomplish your task, and to move out once that force is in the assembly area. We'll call this "min-force" for short. In the above example, it might be two crew-served weapons, two anti-tank weapons, six riflemen, and one radio. Once you have that mix of people and resources in the assembly area, you move out because your min-force has been met. Of course, you leave someone in the assembly area who can bring the rest forward later, because the additional resources will move you to the optimum mix and increase the chances for mission success.

You must have a grasp of the min-force requirements for your job and the things you are managing. Don't wait for the optimum or the perfect amount. As soon as you have the minimum, get to work, and see what you can accomplish. You might get to a point where you can redirect and reallocate resources to other tasks or to other teams. This prevents waste and it keeps your team agile and motivated.

This concept of minimum, optimum, and excess must be applied across two general categories of material that you will manage.

1. The things you produce and/or sell
2. The things you use to help you produce or sell the things you produce or sell

The first category is very specific. If you are making air conditioners or paint, it is the actual HVAC unit or the cans/barrels of paint. If you are selling shoes and apparel, it is the shoes and apparel. We're talking about finished products here and you may not have to manage them for long if you ship them immediately or have high "sell-through," but you must manage them until they leave your control

The second category is very general. This includes all the raw materials, finished components, tools, and expendable items you use to produce your products in and industrial or technology setting. It includes all the fixtures, features, supplies, and equipment used in storing, displaying, and advertising your products in a retail setting.

Understanding what all those things are in the second category is the part that many managers lose sight of. Don't focus exclusively on the first category materials. They are important because they are the end product of your work but managing all the stuff in the second category will enhance your ability to manage the things in the first category.[7]

Tools, Techniques, and Tips for Material Management

1. Inventory

Supplies and stock levels of inventory will drive your success in many fields but often, getting the items you use or sell will be out of your control as a manager. However, once you have them in hand, you need to manage your inventory to know exactly what you have and where to find it when you are ready to use it, deploy it, or sell it.

The problem with inventory is that it requires space to be stored before it can be used or sold. In the case of retail and fashion, aged inventory is unlikely to sell at a premium, so why would you want extra inventory?

Clearly, you must achieve balance between the amount of space you can allocate to storage and the amount of inventory you need to keep on hand for daily, weekly, or even monthly operations. The larger your inventory, the harder it is to find what you need, when you need it. An additional consideration is opportunity costs to holding excess inventory including how else you might use that space.

So really, there are two questions to ask regarding inventory: How much do I need, and how do I keep track of it?

---

[7] I am reminded of an old proverb here which is often used to highlight the impact of small events, but I think it works to highlight the importance of material management: "For the want of a nail the shoe was lost. For the want of a shoe the horse was lost. For the want of a horse the battle was lost. For the failure of battle the kingdom was lost. All for the want of a horse-shoe nail."

Most well-established companies have systems in place to manage inventory such as bar codes, RFID, and point of sale (POS) systems. If you are part of a new company, or a new manager in an established company without an inventory management system in place, this should be your first task for material management.

Knowing what you have "on hand" and where to find it must be a simple and easy process. See the resources page for suggestions on systems and programs you can use to help manage inventory.

2. Hand Receipts and Sub-hand Receipts

Almost a rite of passage, Army officers must sign for all the property in their company when they become a company commander. Approximately one hundred soldiers in size, an Army company is in the low-middle level of management. Platoons and squads below, battalions, brigades, divisions, and ridiculously large formations above, company level is the first official level of command (platoons and squads have "leaders" not "commanders").

Before an officer can take command of his/her company, they must complete a 100 percent inventory of everything on the property book. Depending on the type of company, this can range in value from a few hundred thousand dollars (light infantry company) to tens of millions of dollars (armor and aviation companies).

This process can take days or even weeks to accomplish but once the in-coming commander has seen or touched every accountable piece of equipment, they sign the hand receipt. For all of it. ALL OF IT.

This serves the purpose of letting the new commander understand the magnitude of the material they are now responsible for, but it also instills a sense of ownership and accountability for all the material that belongs to the company and now, the company commander.

As a matter of spreading out the accountability (and the liability) for all the equipment, the commander has platoon leaders sign sub-hand receipts for their portion of the equipment. Platoon leadership in turn have squad leaders and line supervisors sign a sub-hand receipt for their portion. In this way, the responsibility for the security and maintenance is powered down through the chain of command. Again, it serves the dual purpose of building ownership and responsibility in junior leaders.

While you may not have any material that you are signed for, you can use this practice to ensure the people on your team understand the volume and the value of the material they use to perform their work. This can also allow you and them to manage the status of these materials and tools to reorder or replace them as they wear out or break.

3. Joint Inspections

While the "change of command" inventory was done by the in-coming company commander, it was essentially a joint inspection between the old and the new commander of the company's material resources. Wherever accountability is an issue, especially when people on the team are moving up or moving out, a joint inspection/inventory of the material is great idea to protect the company and to protect both members of the team who are relinquishing or establishing accountability for the items. When combined with a transfer of information, this joint inspection can be a vital part of the transition between shift workers in a manufacturing or industrial setting.

If the old and new people cannot conduct the inspection together because of timing or because of other considerations (e.g., social distancing protocols), devise some other way to establish accountability during the transfer. This could include third party verification or some method to check-in/check-out tools and materials.

4. Forecasts

Once you know how much material you have available, you must determine how long it will last and what your lead time is for requesting and receiving more. This is the essence of the forecast, and it's the same if you are keeping the manufacturing processes going or keeping your customers supplied with the freshest fashion. You must forecast your needs, and do it in synch with the order, production, and delivery timelines of your suppliers.

Backward plan from key events or known high-demand periods and use historical data to determine future trends. Every part of the organization involved in the production or sales process must contribute to building the forecast. You must also consider that outside your organization are many sources of data for building your forecasts. Social media can be a great place to see what is trending, and don't forget to check in to see what your competitors are up to. Your suppliers and vendors may also have a better understanding of where the market is headed or where they are having issues sourcing materials.

During periods of abundance, you must understand current and future demands. During periods of scarcity, demand is probably not the problem so your attention and effort must go towards your supply chain and your suppliers.

5. Achieve Effectiveness First; Then Look for Efficiencies

Efficiencies come from doing tasks better, faster, and with less waste. Finding and implementing efficiencies helps mitigate or avoid scarcity and ensures we have all we need. That said, you should never try to achieve efficiencies until you know how to be effective. No amount of efficiency will make up for a lack of effectiveness, i.e., doing the work correctly, safely, and with the highest quality.

With new people, tasks, or material, the quest to be effective may involve a certain amount of trial and error. It will demand training, and it may very well involve a certain amount of "waste" or the expenditure of resources that don't directly impact the bottom line.

You must accept and understand that this is the price of doing business. This begins to cross into the domain of Change Management, but new people, processes, or resources demand our attention to effectiveness. Once your people and your team are effective, then and only then can you look to reduce the time and materials needed to achieve success.

6. Understand the "Burn Rate"

A large part of material management is understanding how quickly you go through your resources. With money, we refer to this as the "burn rate" and we can apply the concept to other material as well. Combined with our understanding of inventory and forecasting, we can manage the burn rate to keep supply levels equal to their rate of use, and to track and program changes in the rates.

One way to manage this is to allocate material evenly over time such as allowing for 8 percent expenditure per month. While this ensures all material is used in the year (96 percent, but the extra 4 percent could be your reserve—see below), it doesn't account for fluctuations in demand.

Apportionment is another strategy to adjust allocation for high use periods. If you anticipate the second half of the year to have 20 percent greater demand than the first half of the year, you can limit material expenditures in the first half to 30 percent (or 15 percent in each of the first two quarters). You can also use historical data to allocate resources based on past demand signals and allocate for each month or period based on what you have seen in the past. Withholding or front-loading material in this way will help prevent a false sense of abundance or scarcity depending on demand.

7. Establish a Reserve

In the military, a reserve force is established to prevent defeat (usually when defending) or to ensure victory (usually when on offense). It can and should be the same in business.

Hold resources in "reserve" to prevent failure or to ensure greater success and establish contingencies and triggers for their use. That is, do not use the reserve until the conditions you established are met and your team executes your plan. That might sound something like this: "Use the reserve if we drop below "x" amount..." or, "Once we achieve "y" amount or better, deploy the extra resources."

8. Supply Chain Verticals

At a strategic level, one of the best ways to ensure you have all the material you need is to secure what is known as the supply chain "vertical." Farm-to-table is a food service example of this. Restaurants that own the farm and the food it produces, the distribution network, and the processing (e.g., butchers) for everything they serve in the restaurant have secured their vertical.

This may not be practical for your organization, but taking charge of as much of your supply chain as possible—if not all—gives you control and certainty of your materials. This is an issue, and these are decision that are "above your pay grade" as a new manager but you do have a role to play that can help your organization better manage the supply chain: you likely have information that your boss does not have.

The information you have and the visibility you have of the trends in your environment may not be known to anyone above you in the organizational chart. If the quality of the items you receive from vendors or suppliers is changing or it is different from one to another, you must pass that information along to your boss. If your clients or customers are looking for or asking for items or features that you don't currently provide, your boss needs to know that too.

If you have the decision authority to act on these trends, you must do so without hesitation but make sure you are communicating that to the people above you in the company.

9. Information and Data

While not historically treated as material, information and data are increasingly important business assets. And just like the physical material in your inventory, you must secure your data when stored or used, know exactly what you have, know exactly where it is, and have timely access to it when needed at the point of use/sale.

While a great deal of data management will depend on the systems and software you use, don't forget there will be people accessing the data to retrieve information or to add new data, so policy and process will matter. How you name files and folders, and how you arrange them in your system will have a significant impact on your team's ability to find and share what they need.

Securing your data must consider threats from outside your organization and account for employee negligence, incompetence, or even mayhem. Negligence and incompetence can be prevented with training, but mayhem happens when disagreement becomes discord. If you hire well, you will not likely encounter the mischief of a disgruntled employee but managing your data means being prepared for this extreme case.

Summary

While all four management domains have an impact on cost, the most obvious and immediate determinate is the cost of resources (material). Your ability to understand what you have, what you need, and how to manage the flow and use of both will not only allow you to be more effective, but it will also eventually bring about efficiencies, reduce costs, and mitigate the impact of supply chain disruptions.

Knowing the difference between what the minimum amount is you need to be successful, versus the optimum or maximum amount, will allow you to be more agile and to move more quickly as you manage between the two. It will also allow you to shift resources to your peers or other parts of your organization when you see that the material you have is more than the optimum amount needed.

CHAPTER 5

RISK MANAGEMENT

"Risk management is a more realistic term than safety. It implies that hazards are ever-present, that they must be identified, analyzed, evaluated, and controlled or rationally accepted."

— Jerome F. Lederer

Risk Defined

The term "risk management" can apply to business and to life in general. If you "Google" the term, you'll probably get this definition from Wikipedia: "Risk management is the identification, evaluation, and prioritization of risks (defined in ISO 31000 as the effect of uncertainty on objectives) followed by coordinated and economical application of resources to minimize, monitor, and control the probability or impact of unfortunate events or to maximize the realization of opportunities."[8]

What I like about this definition is that it includes planning (identification, evaluation, and prioritization) and execution (application of

---

[8] https://en.wikipedia.org/wiki/Risk_management

resources to minimize, monitor, and control). While you may have to deal with the sudden and dangerous risk that "pops up," true risk management is proactive, not reactive. This brings up a third thing I like about this definition: risk management is there for us to mitigate the impact of "unfortunate events," but also to "maximize the realization of opportunities."

Often you will hear people describe risks that appear suddenly as "unintended consequences," and I consider that phrase to be one of the greatest excuses for poor management (and leadership) ever invented. If done properly, risk management will allow you to see or imagine all the threats and all the consequences of your actions or the actions of others in the environment. It takes work, and many managers would rather take their chances and react to unforeseen or unintended circumstances after they happen. Taking this approach to risk management is the business equivalent of medical malpractice.

To think about it another way, we are generally faced with two types of risk: known and unknown. Some analysts take the concept one step further by listing the unknown items as "known unknowns" and "unknown unknowns." Donald Rumsfeld, United States Secretary of Defense under Presidents Ford and Bush (43) is probably the most famous person to address the concept. However you label risk, it is important to remember that you don't know everything, and this is certainly true when it comes to risks in our environment. I mention that here because the impact of the "unknown" in determining condition is most severely seen in this domain of management.

Abundance

The abundance condition of risk will be referred to as "Fearful." This is because, at some point, even the most fearless of us will become fearful when facing extreme risk. When faced with threats, the natural human reaction is one of fight, flight, or freeze. The same is true with risks as they are usually the same as threats, but all three responses can be the physical manifestation of the emotion fear.

Scarcity

A scarcity of risk can lead us to careless behavior, therefore "Reckless" is the name of the extreme condition of risk scarcity. Without risk, or more to the point—without an awareness of risk—the extreme condition would lead to extreme behaviors and ultimately to the point of being reckless. I want to stress again that it's not the risks, but the awareness of risk, that establishes the condition of this domain. Therefore, known and unknown risks must be examined if not imagined in order to shape our actions in risk management.

Which condition are you in and what is the status?

When a task is inherently dangerous, or when the environment is full of threats, it's easy to assess that we are in a condition of abundance. It's also easy to assume greater risk when the task is new, or when the team is new. Ultimately, our capability to deal with specific risks and our capacity to deal with all the risks is what determines our risk management condition.

With scarcity, it is likely that the team and the task are well known and our capabilities and capacities for dealing with risk are well established and well-practiced. That said, complacency is an indicator that you or your team is getting too comfortable with the perceived level of risk. Complacency will breed careless and reckless actions by individuals and the team collectively. If you notice your people becoming too comfortable, there's a good chance they are moving to the scarcity end of the domain and will not see the next risk(s) until it is too late.

General Concepts for Risk Management

While there are countless risks we face in our professional and personal lives, they can all be placed into three distinct categories: risk to mission, risk to personnel, and risk to reputation.

1. Risk to Mission

Any risk that might keep you from accomplishing your assigned tasks should be considered a risk to the mission. The team exists to achieve the mission; you are assigned as a manager to hold them accountable and help them accomplish it. It is your primary and most important job, so "risk to mission" must be your primary concern as you manage in this domain. These risks can range from lack of resources to flaws in design and planning, or to natural and man-made disasters.

2. Risk to Personnel

While most risks to your personnel involve safety and the loss of "life, limb, or eyesight," health and wellness are equally important. Depending on your work setting (e.g., manufacturing plant versus office), these risks to personnel will be more or less prevalent. While secondary (by the smallest of margins) to mission risk, personnel risks take a high priority because they impact your ability to accomplish future missions and they can have a huge impact on your (and the organization's) reputation.

3. Risk to Reputation

The final risk category is risk to reputation. The effects of these risks may be immediate, or they may develop over time, so it is often the last risk we consider in the domain. As mentioned above, how we take care of our people and how we treat them will affect our reputation. How we are perceived in the community, with our clients, customers, and constituents are other manifestations of reputation. Therefore, we must consider both the real and perceived assessments of our character and our purpose.

To manage effectively in this domain, you must identify all the current (known) risks in all three categories, imagine future (known and unknown) risks, and assess your ability to avoid, mitigate, or accept the risk. Your capabilities to deal with risks and your capacity to endure negative impacts will drive your risk tolerance.

Risk tolerance is an important concept because, with most things in life and in business, the greater the risk, the greater the reward. This is not just a mathematical equation; your capability and capacity to manage risks may not address intangible issues like your past history or experience with risk. Even if you have assessed your current abilities and capacities as large or significant, if you cannot get over a previous bad experience with risk management, your risk tolerance will be lower than your capabilities suggest.

We must also remember that personal risk tolerance is not the same as organizational risk tolerance. You may be very comfortable with risk, and as a result, you may take more aggressive actions or investments. Your organization, historically or culturally, might have a totally different view of risk and a much lower tolerance level. If you miss that distinction and take aggressive actions and risks in the company's name, you may encounter huge push-back from your boss and your peers when the company culture is more risk-averse. Even if you succeed, you may damage your reputation in the organization.

Risk management together with the associated actions of risk avoidance, risk mitigation, or acceptance is therefore not a wholly mechanistic process. It requires attention to planning and execution; capabilities and capacities to deal with risk; and an understanding of personal and organizational tolerance for risk.

For all these reasons, the subject of risk and successfully dealing with it is an issue that is part management and part leadership. I won't dig too deep on this topic here because this is a central element of my next book. For now, let me continue with some tools, techniques, and tips that apply in a general sense to all organizations and managers who want to better understand and manage risk.

Tools, Techniques, and Tips for Risk Management

1. Absolute Standards

Whether we are talking about mission accomplishment or personnel safety, you likely have processes and procedures in place to mitigate the risks to each. These may include quality assurance checks or personal protective equipment (PPE). Because these things will likely be specific to your work, there's no need to address specifics here, except that as a manager you need to ensure whatever those processes and procedures are, that they are being done fully and completely.

This means that you cannot have shifting or relative standards. You must have absolute standards and ensure that those standards are being met by everyone on your team. Certainly, if conditions change or if new materials or processes emerge, your risk exposure may change and so your standards must change. This can go both ways, where you relax your standards or raise your standards.

The bottom line is this: whatever the risks and whether they are abundant or scarce, your team must adhere to the standard that you or the organization (your boss) have set. Failure to meet or exceed the standard will lead to negative outcomes, even if only that your team feels like they don't have to do what they were told because the consequences of not performing or adhering to the standard are nonexistent.

2. Red Lines and Trip Wires

Certainly, with the risks we have identified, we can and should establish a threshold of failure that must not be crossed. However, we must also identify measures and indicators of increasing danger that initiate actions that avoid, mitigate, or accept specific risks. The first is called a "red line" and the second a "trip wire."

In planning for risk, you must first establish or understand your "red lines." These are absolute standards or conditions that your team cannot venture into. Establish them for all three of the major risk categories (mission, people, and reputation) and make sure everyone knows what they are.

In practice, trip wires always precede red lines, and while there can be more than one trip wire for each red line, each trip wire should initiate or activate (or stop) one process, action, or procedure. The beauty of effectively communicated trip wires is that when they are well established and well known by the entire team, the decisions related to risk have already been made; all the team needs to do is execute those decisions. When used properly, the team will move faster and with greater confidence.

This is true with a scarcity of risk as much as with an abundance of risk. Establish trip wires and red lines even when there is seemingly little or no risk. This will guard against complacency. It will give you something you can rehearse with your team, even if only a discussion (If "x" happens, we immediately do "y"), and when the level of risk in the environment suddenly shifts from scarce to abundant, you will be ready.

3. Reconnaissance and Rehearsals

One of the most impactful lessons I learned early on as a soldier is the value of reconnaissance and rehearsal. Military history is full of examples of success and failure. The most common element of successful units versus unsuccessful units is the time and quality of their reconnaissance of the enemy and the terrain where they must fight, and the time and quality of their rehearsals to defeat that enemy on that terrain. The better the reconnaissance and rehearsal, the greater the probability of success.

In January and February of 1991, the 2nd Brigade of the 82nd Airborne Division was attached to the 6th French Light Armored Division on the far western (left) flank of the coalition forces assembled to defeat the Iraqi Army and liberate Kuwait. For two months we engaged in a mix of reconnaissance and counter-reconnaissance operations to determine the strength and location of the Iraqi forces and to prevent them from learning the same things about us.

My company was on the screen line while the rest of my battalion was some distance behind us. The other two battalions in the brigade were arrayed in a similar fashion. During the day we lay hidden but kept observers up looking for Iraqi troop movements. At night we conducted reconnaissance of the escarpment we would have to traverse/scale and the enemy positions we would assault when the ground campaign started.

We were under strict rules to not talk on our radios, least the Iraqis intercept the signals which they could use to determine our strength and location and then direct artillery fire on us. That meant that we communicated using field telephones connected to wires that we rolled out from large spools. Every night my scout teams would ride out to a drop-off point, running wire from my command post. At the drop-off point, they would continue to run wire from smaller spools they carried as they climbed the escarpment mapping out routes for the rest of the battalion to follow, and then conduct reconnaissance of the enemy positions at the top.

This was a risky operation that required stealth. It also required us to recover our wire every night so the enemy wouldn't find it. Had we left it behind, we would have saved a lot of time for the next night's reconnaissance, but it would have been easy for the Iraqis to set up an ambush on the wire and hit us as we moved into position along the wire the next night.

My boss (the battalion commander) didn't like this process because our scout teams were only getting an hour or two of reconnaissance on top of the escarpment each night while the other two battalions were getting four or five hours of reconnaissance in the same period of darkness. I told the battalion commander that the other battalions must be leaving their wire out, and that this practice was stupid, showing poor tactics. I also told the battalion commander I would not do the same thing as it was far too risky. Instead, I ensured our scouts rehearsed deploying and recovering the wire as part of their daily routine before the nightly missions as a way to ensure we were as efficient as possible in that task, giving them more time for reconnaissance.

It was not more than two nights after my commander came to me, complaining about the disparity in time spent conducting reconnaissance and asking me to have the scouts leave their wire out each night, that 4th Battalion's scouts were ambushed by an Iraqi patrol that had found the wire they had left behind.

Fortunately for 4th Battalion's scouts, they got into the kill zone of the ambush site about the same time the Iraqis were setting up. No one was killed or wounded, and my commander came to me the next day with something that was close to an apology, but not really.

As a manager, for the benefit of your team and for your own benefit, find the time to conduct reconnaissance of the place where you do your work or business, especially when you are putting in a new process or new equipment. Look at how everything works together and how your people will operate with or within this new set-up. You will likely find risks you didn't know about or that the things you thought were risky aren't really that big of a threat—or perhaps they are an even greater threat. No matter, it pays huge dividends to go and see things for yourself.

The reconnaissance you do will also help you conduct better rehearsals. Like putting out wire and recovering it each night, rehearsals will allow you to see and understand your processes and how they work in the real world, not just on the drawing board. Make your rehearsals as realistic as possible, but if you only have time and material to have a discussion with your team, do that. Use a picture of the area if you can't walk the area. Never let a lack of resources, especially time, keep you from doing a rehearsal.

4. Conduct a "Pre-Mortem"

I'm a big fan of capturing lessons learned after every event, both when we succeed and when we fail. In the Army, we called this the "After-Action Review" (AAR). In the medical profession, especially if someone dies during a procedure, they "AAR" conducted to understand what went wrong is known as a "post-mortem."

With risk, we often can't wait to learn the lessons after the fact. We need to know if we can accept, mitigate, or avoid the risks that are out there. But how can we do that before the fact? One way is to conduct a "pre-mortem."

Bring together your team and any other experts who have insights into the process, procedures, and capabilities (think safety, quality, and maintenance experts as an example). Now, imagine that you have just failed at your mission. What would that look like? What are the possible risks or points of weakness that would cause you to fail or for someone to get injured?

Now work backward from those risks and events and determine what you can or should do differently to avoid or to mitigate the failure. You will likely see the need for new safeguards or different sequencing of events as you conduct your "pre-mortem."

If you find yourself in an abundant condition for risk, you might think that you don't have time for this, but you need to make time. You need to break out of the tendency to only react to the risks that occur and get in front of them before they happen. You can plan for success, but you can never assume success. Part of your planning must include the possibilities of risk or failure. Think about it now (it's a type of mental reconnaissance) and work through the ways to prevent or lessen it.

When you are in the scarcity condition for risk, remember that it may only be your perception and not fact. A pre-mortem will help you understand the true level of risk, it will help you keep your team focused and not complacent, and it will prepare you and them for a shift in risk conditions from scarcity (reckless) to abundant (fearful).

5. Ask Better Questions: "What are we missing?"

Another way to manage risk is to assign someone the task of questioning your thinking and your processes. This person might be referred to as a "Devil's Advocate,"[9] but it doesn't have to be that contentious. You simply need someone to remind you and your team to think more critically.

You can kick-start better thinking by asking better questions. Some of the best questions for risk management are simple: "What are we missing?" or "What else could go wrong?"

While anyone on the team can (and should) ask these questions, assigning the task to one individual will assure it gets done. Rotate the duty amongst your people so they all get the chance to fill this role.

---

[9] Generally, a person who takes an opposing position for the sake of argument or to force more discussion.

In this way they will be thinking about the questions as much as the answers. Over time, everyone on your team will naturally ask these kinds of questions that dig deeper into the processes, procedures, and actions we take, as well as the risks that we know and the risks that we don't know.

6. Empowerment

Empowering your people is a great way to mitigate risk. Not because you pass the risk along to them, but because you give them the tools to see, decide, act, and react to risks and problems that come into play during operations.

It is important, however, that you don't just say to your people, "I'm empowering you to do this…" If you don't ensure the "3R's" of empowerment, you will be setting them up for failure and you will be assuming more risk both for yourself and your organization.

The 3 Rs of empowerment: Ready, Resource, and Responsibility

The first "R" is "Ready." Ensure the person you have chosen is ready, willing, and able to handle the authority and power you are about to give them. Ask yourself these questions: Are they mature enough (ready)? Do they have the right mindset (willing)? And do they have the right skill set (able)? It's your job to assess them for all three and help them where you can, most often in training them to build their skillset. The confidence that comes with greater skills will build their mindset as well.

The second "R" is "Resource." Ensure you have given them all the resources needed to be empowered. Time, material, and authority come most easily to mind, but don't forget to communicate to the rest of your team and anyone else that has a stake in the overall success of the team (clients, vendors, other teams within the company) that this person is now empowered to do (fill in the blank) the things you have authorized them to do.

The final "R" is "Responsibility." While you can and should empower your people to the best of your and their ability, remember that while you can give them authority for a task or a problem, the responsibility for getting it accomplished is, and always will be, your own.

When there is an abundance of risk, you might think that you cannot afford to empower people to make the decisions or to take the actions needed, but this is actually the best time to empower your people— provided you use the 3 Rs.

And if there is a scarcity of risk, all the better for your people to learn and grow into a more empowered role. You may need to set up training scenarios that imply "risk" to allow them to really grow into the role. Do this training similar to how you do a rehearsal or a pre-mortem.

7. Challenge Comfort Zones

As I said earlier, complacency is the greatest indicator that your people don't appreciate the risks in the environment. It may be the case that there is currently little or no risk, but if you allow it, the attitudes, habits, and behaviors your people develop will far outlast the scarcity condition.

So, before your condition for risk shifts from scarcity to abundance, and to keep your people from becoming reckless, challenge their comfort zones. Give them training scenarios where you inject failures or problems. How do they react? Set up red lines and trip wires and see if they recognize them and if they act accordingly. Conduct an AAR and don't let anyone off the hook; everyone must reflect and learn from both failure and success. Let them appreciate risks, but let them develop the real skills to avoid, mitigate, or accept risk in a safe and measured way.

You can also take your personnel out of the work environment to do something that is challenging and that will push the limits of their comfort zone. Zip lines and ropes courses are a popular option here. Obstacle courses and races like "Tough Mudder" or "Spartan" can do the same, but make sure everyone is physically fit and medically sound before doing something that challenging.

Summary

One of the greatest examples of effective risk management that I can think of is the National Geographic movie *Free Solo*. This documentary captures the planning, preparation, and accomplishment of Alex Honnold as he became the first human to climb the 2,900-foot tall "Freerider" route of El Capitan without a rope or any other assistance. The risks were astronomical, certainly to his person, but also to his reputation and to the reputation of the film crew. He succeeded in part because he assessed the known risks, planned for possible unknown risks, and then mitigated the risks through detailed planning, reconnaissance, and rehearsals. His ability to disassociate himself from the environment and focus on what was right in front of him is extraordinary, but the techniques he used to mitigate the risks and accomplish his mission can be copied by anyone whether your mountain is real or metaphorical.

CHAPTER 6

CHANGE MANAGEMENT

"Your success in life isn't based on your ability to simply change. It is based on your ability to change faster than your competition, customers, and business."

— Mark Sanborn

Change Defined

Change can be both a verb and a noun; in the first case, it describes the action and in the second case the end state. While we must be concerned with the outcome of each action and decision we make as managers, our discussion here will center on the verb form of the word.

I think the most fitting definitions relative to management highlight how change can be minor or significant. According to Merriam-Webster:

a: to make different in some particular way: ALTER

b: to make radically different: TRANSFORM

c: to give a different position, course, or direction to

Managers are called on to design, plan, and implement any of the above three changes. The change may be directed by their own initiative, by their boss or senior leadership, or by stakeholders internal (employees) or external (customers) to their team.

Regardless of the source of the idea or request for change, there are two types of change that you will need to manage. The first is something we do to stay even with or to get ahead of trends and technology. We generally call this innovation. The second is the change that we are often forced to do just to stay relevant, or even to survive. We might call this change remedial or reactionary.

Abundance

The abundance condition of change management is "Volatility." At the extreme, abundant change is volatile and it becomes nearly impossible to keep up with the change, let alone to get ahead of it. If this is your condition, you must have agile systems and routines that allow you and your team to adjust on the fly.

Scarcity

While a scarcity of change might seem like a good thing, it often ends in ruin. Therefore, I refer to the extreme of this condition as "Fossilization." If you don't ever change, or if you are ignorant to the need for change, you will become a dinosaur, and then a fossil. The history of the last half-century is full of stories that end this way. When Sears, Kodak, or Blockbuster were dominant in their fields, they seemed to not sense a need for change, or they missed the chance to make the changes that would allow them to continue to prosper. All three are now relics of the past and exist like fossils, a reminder of giants that once roamed the business world.

Which condition are you in and what is the status?

The volatility that comes with an extreme abundance of change is characterized by sharp, rapid, and unpredicted changes. We often think of this as a large and sudden downturn in the financial markets, but it also describes sudden upturns. While it's human nature to fixate on the negative, remember that when we are in a condition of abundant change (financial or otherwise), so is everyone else. A key in dealing with volatility is to embrace the changes and find opportunities that can allow you to excel relative to the competition who may fear making decisions under volatile conditions.

A scarcity of change is the opposite. When everything seems constant, or when change appears predictable and minor, we become comfortable with our situation and our surroundings. It's not very exciting and we forget to look for innovation opportunities to prepare for the future. This is what we might call a velvet rut—we stay happy and comfortable, but we are in a hole. If you find yourself comfortable or even bored, you are most likely in the scarcity condition of change.

General Concepts for Change Management

Once you identify a need to change, or once you have been told/directed to make a change, there are general concepts to successfully manage.

First and foremost, the decision to change is simply a decision. Like all decisions, you must begin knowing two things with full certainty: 1) What is the objective or outcome you want to achieve? 2) How much time do you have to achieve it? If you cannot answer these two questions, you will be lost and your attempts to manage change (this decision) will likely fail or fall well short of expectation. More than any other factors, the objective and time allotted will drive you in managing all change.

Once you know your objective and the time allocated, you must follow a change management process. The one I offer here is Plan, Measure, combat Resistance, Learn, Assess (PMRLA).

Plan: This is your general concept for the change you are enacting and how you will achieve a successful outcome. There are two specific strategies within this part of PMRLA: the first is your Implementation and Training Plan, and the second is your Communication Plan

Implementation and Training (I&T) Plans are exactly that—how will you implement this change and what training must you provide for your people, customers, or other stakeholders?

The Communication Plan comes after you develop the I&T Plan because it is one of the main things you must communicate to the team, and anyone else affected by the change.

Measure: Once you have planned for and implemented the change, you will need to measure your progress. The metrics you choose will probably include some items that measure performance (e.g., how much money spent) and some items that measure effectiveness (e.g., customer satisfaction). With this step, you must know what you are looking at or looking for, and where to find such data.

Resistance: Change of all types is usually met with varying degrees of resistance by some members of the team or community. The resistance might be mild and disorganized, or it might be intense and well connected. From experience we can anticipate who might resist this change and why they are resistant.

The first people who might resist change are folks who are invested in the old way of doing things. This includes the people who planned, developed, or implemented the old way. These people resist change because they have ego and emotions tied up in the old way. They often feel diminished and not valued when the system or process they developed is changed. Others resist the change because their job or job title is connected to the old way. They fear change because it might mean a demotion, firing, or early retirement.

The second group of people who might resist are those who are opposed to the new way. Their opposition might stem from ignorance, or it might stem from principle. Ignorance means they simply don't know or don't see the value in the change; principle means that they believe the new way runs counter to their beliefs.

Another group that is likely to resist change is people who have had a bad experience with change. Their resistance may come from a lack of trust in management. That might be a lack of trust in previous managers (who might have been promoted and are now your boss), or it might be a lack of trust in you.

The final category of resistance comes from people who, quite frankly, are lazy. They resist change because change often requires additional work. It may require new skills and new attitudes or mindsets; neither of these things tend to go over well with lazy people. Ironically, they usually put more effort into resistance and not changing than what the change itself would require.

In all cases, you must educate the resisters or allay their concerns with your communication plan, and you must follow-up with them regularly. More on how to combat resistance in the next section.

Learn: Learning comes from observation and a willingness to admit we don't know everything there is to know. As you are working through your change plan, you must be willing to recognize where you are succeeding and where you are not. You must keep your eyes, ears, and mind open always, and with all the people implementing the change or impacted by it.

Assess: As you learn things about the processes, systems, structures, and other elements of this change, you must assess where you are and what more (or less) you should do to achieve your desired outcome. Questions you should always ask yourself include: "Is this working?" "What can we do better?" and "What else needs to change?" Even when you achieve the outcome you wanted, you must assess the question of "What's next?" The next change is coming; it may be a minor tweak, or it may be a major transformation. Even (or especially) if you think this latest change has been so successful that you have moved from a condition of change abundance to change scarcity, you must continually assess the need for any future change.

Tools, Techniques, and Tips for Change Management

1. Leader's Intent Statements

Known as "Commander's Intent" in the military, this brief statement of intent allows subordinates in the organization to use their initiative to achieve results if the situation changes. It's both a tool to manage change and to empower your team to work independently rather than constantly having to come back to you for advice or a new decision.

There are three elements to a leader's intent statement: Purpose, Key Tasks, and End State.

Purpose lets your team understand why they are doing what you told them to do, and why it's important. The impact on the company, the customers, and the community all can be a part of this declaration of purpose. This allows everyone to buy into the work or task at hand.

Key tasks allow you to prioritize the things that your people must do to accomplish the work or project. You should limit this to five or less, but certainly cover all the tasks that are essential to a successful outcome.

Finally, the intent statement should address how you see the team when they have finished. At a minimum, you should talk about where they as individuals and as a team should be relative to other parts of the company, the marketplace, and the competition. (See the resources section for an example of a "Leader's Intent" statement)

2. Implementation/Training Planning

Any implementation and training plan must begin with a clear understanding of objective: what is it we are trying to accomplish or to be with this change? This comes from the fundamentals of decision making because change is implemented as the result of some decision. Therefore, it's of critical importance that you know your objective before you ever start.

Following the objective, and again from the fundamentals of decision making, you must know how much time you need to implement this change and achieve your objective.

The next part of your implementation planning must address any new/ additional skills that your team will need, and if that will require special training. In fact, the change itself may be a new process or new tools and equipment that they have never used before, or never used in a new way. Here, you have two options depending on the time, resources, and task; you can do the training on the job, or you can conduct specific and separate training. In the first case, you will be able to let your team "learn as they go" in the actual environment where they work and where the change will take place. If, however, the training requires specific tools or limited resources, you may need to train your people in a central location. There are advantages and disadvantages to each method, so choose the one that works best for you and your people.

Once you have identified the training or other activities needed to implement the change, "backward plan" the training or activities from the due or finished date. This allows you to see any places where you must compress activities or do them in tandem. The Gantt Charts and CPM we discussed in the Time Management chapter are useful here.

As you work through your planning and implementation of this change, remember that you must work to be effective before you can begin to find efficiencies. Looking to be efficient before you are effective is a waste of time and resources.

3. Communication Planning

Remember, you must communicate your plan for impending change as soon as possible.

Once your implementation plan is complete, you must share it with your team and any other stakeholders that have a need to know. Consider multiple channels of communication; different communication preferences among your team members (visual, auditory, reading, kinesthetic) demand this, and each system or platform has advantages and disadvantages (email, phone, collaborative tools, etc.) that allow you to be the most clear and concise. It's important to consider too that your team will have questions and they will want to share those with you or the person(s) you have put in charge of implementing the change. If possible, deliver the implementation plan in person.

In addition to the details of how the change will be implemented, you must communicate why it is important. This could be the statement of purpose you used in your "Leader's Intent," or it could include other benefits and features of the change. This should also be geared to addressing the people and the sources of resistance to the change.

Work repetition into the communication plan and use multiple channels to ensure your message is received and understood. This is important: never assume you are understood. Ask questions of your team that require thought and consideration of what you just communicated and get them to tell you the tasks and outcomes in their own words. You should also plan for updates to the team as you make progress and advance towards your objective. These updates should be both routine, as in thirty, sixty, or ninety days into the implementation plan, or they can be based on contingencies, as in: it's not working and we need to change again...

And finally, make yourself available to listen to your team members. Their feedback and concerns will help you better understand the impact and effects of the change on the organization, and on them.

4. Network Diagrams

Because resistance to change is natural and inevitable, you must address it directly. Diagraming a network is a technique used in the military to visualize and understand how different networks communicate and operate. This can be a very elaborate process done by hand or by using commercial software. However, we're not looking for military precision here. Our purpose in using a network diagram is to better understand the dynamics in our team/organization, and to better see who can be a positive influence and who might be resistant.

This will allow you to anticipate who might be resistant to the change you need to implement, why they are resistant, and who else in the network (your organization or teams) can influence them to be accepting of the change.

You can do this simply by making a list that identifies resisters, influencers, and connectors: people that can work across different networks or parts of networks. We've addressed which groups of people might resist change earlier in this chapter. After you list likely resisters, list the people who can influence them and who are likely to be supportive or positive about the change. Work with these people first before you go directly to the resisters. It's also a good idea to have your influencers help with the communications planning and messaging.

You want to identify the people, but you want to give your attention and effort to addressing the issues causing their resistance. Ultimately you may have to remove those people from the team if they continue to resist, but your first duty is to address the sources of resistance.

5. Understanding the Front-Side and Back-Side of Decision Making

The Front Side of Decision Making:

The following elements constitute the "front side" of decision making. Knowing them and understanding how they work will help you develop and select better choices and make better decisions, and they are especially important in making changes.

Process Constraints: Keep a running list of your available resources, a list of things you must do, and a list of things you cannot do. This involves rules and regulations, as well as any available or mandatory protocols and systems.

Information: This is the lifeblood of decision making, but understand that you will never have complete or perfect information—if you did, the decision would be obvious, and your job would end here. Get people to push you the information you need and learn to go after and pull in the information you want.

Innovations: Are there new ways to use the resources you have or are there new resources out there that could give you more options? Follow the trends and innovations in your line of work or your business. Leverage them to your advantage in making decisions that will put you ahead of the competition.

Judgement: Combined with the analysis of what you gather in the above three areas, your judgement is the ultimate tool in decision making. Use your experience and the experience of trusted advisors to define and then select the best options.

Once you have worked through all four of the above elements, you are ready to decide, or to recommend a decision to your boss. Like anything else, it takes understanding and practice to get good at the "front side" of decision making. Get comfortable with this process and in time you'll get faster and better at it. But remember too that the decision is not the end of the process; at best you are only half-way through. Effectively using the "front-side" process will allow you to choose better options and more importantly, you'll be in a better position on the "back side" of the decision too.

The Back Side of Decision Making:

Outcomes always trump the process. Other than issues of law and ethics, it doesn't matter how you achieve your objective; it only matters if you succeed or fail. Therefore, the "back side" of your decision is very important and yet we often forget this once the decision is made. Below are the components of what I mean by the "back-side" of decision making.

Information: Just as you need information to decide, you need information to monitor the outcomes of your decision. Make sure you have a system in place to observe, monitor, and report on the progress and/or impacts of your decisions. This leads you to "confirmation."

Confirmation: Regardless of the decision, the outcome will fall into one of two categories: success or failure. You need to know what each look like so you can act or react as quickly as possible to either exploit success or to mitigate failure. Beware of confirmation bias (when you only look for the signs of success) and, importantly, beware of your pride. Each can get in the way of seeing and then acting on failure.

Exploit Success: You need to develop a plan to exploit the outcomes and impacts of a successful decision. If you are waiting for signs of success before developing this plan, you are already too late. You must envision success and plan your next steps in the "front side" before you move forward.

Mitigate Failure: Just like exploiting success, you need a plan to fix things when your decision is not going as well as it should or as well as you would like. Recognize that mitigating failure runs the spectrum from a minor adjustment to a complete overhaul. And just like your plan to exploit success, your plan to mitigate failure must be developed before you start to enact the decision or the change.

Learn, Share, Grow: Whether you succeed or fail, you must capture the lessons learned from the experience and the process. Without reflection and review, you will likely continue to make the same mistakes or continue to rely on luck. The "back side" is never finished until you conduct an after-action review. Have a plan to capture, store, and then retrieve these lessons so you can put them to work in the front-side of your next decision.

6. Attitude

Your personal example is your most potent tool as a leader and as manager. And more than what you say or do, your attitude will be what people remember the most and will have the greatest influence in the successful implementation of change.

It's vitally important that you have a positive attitude, and your attitude must also reflect realism. People will appreciate your honesty and candor about any difficulties and risks associated with the change. Don't use phony optimism or a cavalier attitude as both will erode trust and contribute to resistance.

7. What to do when "what always worked" doesn't work anymore

You may have awesome systems and programs to help you accomplish your mission. And as leader, you might have been the person who created or approved that program. That means you probably have a vested interest (and possibly some ego) in keeping that program.

But the nature of the world is that things are constantly changing, and the things that don't or cannot change often get left behind. So, what to do when a system or program you have, that has worked so well in the past, isn't working so well now?

<u>Lose the ego</u>. Recognize that as smart as you are, you might be missing something, or you might have too much emotion tied up in the system or the program that isn't performing like it used to. This sounds easy and obvious, but it can be hard if we have a blind spot to the need for change.

<u>Assemble a team of "experts."</u> Gather the people you trust to assess current technologies and trends. Make sure all have an opportunity to state their opinion and ideas. And most importantly, bring together the smart people who build and design these things, and the smart people who will use the system or the process—they know what they need and what works in the "real world."

<u>Create three bins</u>. As you evaluate the current system, don't throw it all away just because it doesn't work like it used to. The problem(s) are likely with some part or parts, not the whole.

- Things that are working well and we should keep. This is where your end-users can be very helpful.

- Things that aren't working well but could be modified. Your experts will be able to see the realm of possibility in terms of modifications and the cost of making a change.

- Things that aren't working well and should be scrapped. Ideally, these things should be obvious, but getting rid of them can be hard if there is emotion or ego tied up in them.

Change is a constant in our lives, but it doesn't have to be radical. Keep an open mind to what works and what doesn't work. Make changes and modifications on the margins and get input from the people who build the systems and from those who use them.

Summary

Change is an ever-present part of life and business. Be open to the need for change and innovation so that you and your team can continue to grow. Look for any deviations in the environment that you must react to, and work to get out in front of them. Once you've identified a need to change your processes, systems, or activities, get clear on your objective and what you intend to accomplish with the change. Use a system like PMRLA to plan, measure, and learn as you work through the change.

CHAPTER 7

CONCLUSIONS

Like it or not, you are part of the succession plan in your organization. Especially in hierarchical organizations, you're being evaluated, and the leadership is asking one question: "Does this person have the potential and the ability to do more in our organization?"

That question is close-ended—meaning, it can be answered with a simple "yes" or "no." The answer will determine your path and your longevity with the organization.

If "no" is the answer, you can continue to work as a valued "individual contributor," but only for as long as the company can afford to pay you in that limited role. Even without a promotion, you will get cost of living and longevity pay increases, and before long, you become an overpaid individual contributor. You are taking up space for someone new who might have the capacity and desire to do more in the company. That makes them more valuable, and it makes you an expense the company may not want to continue paying for. Over time, the answer to the question might become a "yes," but it's more likely you will be released into the job market.

If, however, the answer is "yes," then understand that you are part of the succession planning. The senior leadership may not have the time, energy, skill, or money to invest in your development, so like Donna

Frazier, you might be left on your own to figure out how to become "management."

In the Army, we used to jokingly say: "No good deed goes unpunished." Sadly, it is true that many organizations will "reward" their best performers by working them to death.

However, hard work and accomplishing your mission do come with many rewards. The first is esteem, and the satisfaction that comes with the knowledge of a job well done. The second is monetary, and it comes in the form of pay raises and bonuses. The third is promotion, and that too comes with a pay raise, but also a new title and added responsibility with more demands on your time, effort, energy, and the need to produce more success.

If promotions and a management title are your objective, you are thrilled with the prospects of being in the "yes" group. But if you are reluctant to step into a manager's role, what are your choices? You could start looking for a new job, one that won't ask you to take it on as a career with advancement but will allow you to just do the job; you can wait for the inevitable promotion to happen and hope for the best; or you can get active in your growth and development to be successful as a manager in your organization.

The choice is yours, but since you are reading this book, I will assume you have decided the third option from those above.

In addition to the tools, techniques, and tips listed in the chapters of this book, what should you do when you find yourself on the horns of this dilemma?

Study. Dig deeper into the techniques and methods mentioned in this book or in other blogs or forums that talk about management. You'll notice that I didn't use cost, scope, or schedule as management domains, yet these are commonly used in management certification programs.

I didn't use those terms because I believe, especially with cost, that they are driven and determined in many cases by the essential domains I have identified in the pages of this book. That said, if you want to learn more about them specifically, seek out opportunities online or from different institutions of higher education. You don't need to enroll in an MBA program; most colleges and universities award certificates in management with weekend programs for people like you who have day jobs.

And of course, the internet is a great source of information that includes pictures, videos, lectures, and exercises, allowing you to move beyond reading about management.

Observe. Observe other managers in your organization. See which are good at doing these things and which struggle. Take notes and ask questions to see what tips and techniques they find helpful in your field. And remember that you can learn as much (if not more) from failures as you can from success. Better to learn from the success and failures of other people.

Select. As you observe the managers around you, select a mentor who can guide you along your path. You may seek coaching or ask your boss to provide a coach to assist in your development, but a coach is not necessarily a mentor.

Coaches can be assigned to you, but you select a mentor. The mentor must be someone you want to emulate. That is a very personal decision, so a mentor cannot be assigned or selected for you. Coaching helps with the development of skills and attributes specific to what you are trying to accomplish. Mentoring is more generally about your career and your path, as a manager and as a person.

Once you find someone who you want to be your mentor, approach them with confidence but also with respect for their time and energy. Observation will likely be your best way to learn from your mentor, but in time you should engage them with questions and ask them to do more with you as their time and schedule allows.

And this is something I think is cool—you never have to tell them they are your mentor, at least not right away. If they are doing things well, they have probably been selected by other people to be a mentor. They probably know this too, but it's not why they are doing what they do, it's just an added benefit. Some of the best moments of my career were when someone who used to work for me approached me years after the fact and told me what a positive impact I had on them and their career—that I was a mentor to them.

Read more. If you made it this far, you already know this, and it is my greatest hope that you have learned a thing or two. I would also recommend that if you haven't already, read my first book, *Leadership in Balance*.

Leadership is much more personal than management. The former is "art" while the latter is "science." Leadership and how you lead your team are impacted by your natural tendencies and what the situation demands from you; the secret to success is your ability to balance those two things

Management, in contrast, is agnostic to your tendencies and affected by the conditions present for each domain. Balance comes from the manager's ability to prevent movement to the extreme version of abundance or scarcity, and his/her ability to prepare for the opposite condition as abundance and scarcity tend to run in cycles.

Ultimately you will have to learn how to both lead and manage your team, and to that end, I am already working on my next book. Keep an eye out for my third book, *Solving the Leader's Dilemma: Finding the Balance between Leadership and Management*, due out in late spring or early summer of 2023. You can also follow me on social media or visit my website, bethefulcrum.com, to sign up for email notifications.

ACKNOWLEDGEMENTS

First and foremost, I'd like to acknowledge the love and support of my family. In every success they are the foundation of what I've been able to achieve. Martha, DELFP, HC, my mother and father, my brother and sister and their spouses, and all my in-laws; thank you and I love you.

I also want to acknowledge my clients who, over the past five years, have made me better at what I love to do. Coaching, training, instructing, and facilitating to help them grow and to help them solve their problems, this post-Army life is more than I could ever imagine thanks to them. Particular mention is due for the team at Hibbett | City GEAR (Hibbett Inc.); their passion for what they do and their desire to improve every day inspires me in ways too numerous to recount here. You'll learn more about them, their CEO Mike Longo, and their leadership team in my next book.

Finally, I want to acknowledge the composite of people I have encountered and observed over the last fifteen years who inspired me to write about the "reluctant manager." I hope this book, paired with *Leadership in Balance*, gives them (you) the tools and inspiration you need to be amazing in your management/leadership role.

ABOUT THE AUTHOR

Credit: Emma Hope Photography

Michael Lerario

Mike Lerario is President and Principal Consultant for Crispian Consulting Inc., a firm that provides specialized training and coaching in Leadership Development and organizational effectiveness. Additionally, Mike serves as subject matter expert on numerous research projects for the Army and the Department of Defense.

A 1983 graduate of the United States Military Academy, Mike served 23 years as an Infantry Officer in Airborne Ranger assignments and retired a Lieutenant Colonel in 2006 after serving with the Joint Special Operations Command.

Mr. Lerario's Army career includes command assignments through battalion level and staff assignments as operations officer at battalion, brigade, and joint staff levels. He has multiple combat tours in both Afghanistan and Iraq.

Following his retirement from active duty, Mr. Lerario worked as an Operational Advisor with the U.S. Army Asymmetric Warfare Group (AWG) and with NATO training "Attack the Network" and

Counterinsurgency (COIN) Operations. He returned to Afghanistan in 2013 to assist in the training and development of the Afghan National Army Special Operations Command (ANASOC) and in 2014 to serve as Senior Command Advisor to the three-star commanding general of all NATO operational forces in Afghanistan.

He holds a Bachelor of Science in Engineering (with a concentration in Military History) and a Master of Art in Leadership Development, both degrees from the United States Military Academy at West Point, NY.

Mike is the author of the 2016 Amazon.com International Best Seller *Leadership in Balance: The Fulcrum-Centric Plan for Emerging and High Potential Leaders. Management in Balance: The Fulcrum-Centric Plan for New and Reluctant Managers* is a companion to his first book, defining management and establishing a contrast to leadership. His next book, *Solving the Leader's Dilemma: Finding the Balance between Management and Leadership*, is scheduled for publication in the summer of 2023.

ADDITIONAL RESOURCES

Time Management

There are many resources for Gantt Charts, but obviously, the first to capitalize on that URL name is gantt.com. This is where I found the Matchware software that I use to make Gantt charts, but you will also find other resources for project management, workflow, business plans, and SWOT analysis. To be clear, you will have to pay for this software. I am neither a paid spokesperson or representative of this company, but I have purchased, and I do use their product.

https://www.gantt.com/

Written in 1963 by F. K. Levy, G. L. Thompson, and J. D. Wiest, this article in the Harvard Business Review should be considered an original source for Critical Path Method (CPM). It is clear, concise, and has charts and graphs to help explain "The ABCs of the Critical Path Method."

https://hbr.org/1963/09/the-abcs-of-the-critical-path-method

Taking notes using paper and pen or keeping "to-do" lists is much easier when you can carry a notebook or note cards with you. Long before PDAs and smartphones were a thing, I used a monthly calendar book with two pages per day. The brand I used was called "Day-Timer" and it was a graduation gift from my brother Tom. I don't currently use their products, but I found it very useful when I did.

https://www.daytimer.com/

Another company that has a great assortment of products for taking notes and keeping track of tasks is Levenger. I currently travel with a "pocket briefcase" that I use to hold business cards, identification, and note cards that I can use whenever my phone is not appropriate. It's a very professional bit of gear that provides a professional look.

https://www.levenger.com/

Though not specifically about time management, *The Big Leap* by Gay Hendricks[10] discusses the difference between a Newtonian concept of time (time is scarce) and an Einstein concept of time (time is created by us) in chapter six. How we look at time, as finite or infinite, drives us to stay where we are comfortable, or allows us to take the big leap into our zones of genius.

Because Kevin Kruse's book *15 Secrets Successful People Know About Time Management*[11] involves a collection of interviews of successful people from a wide range of activities, you are very likely to find something in this book that you can use in your life, both personally and professionally.

A final book on time management that I recommend is one of the best for a perspective on what we say "yes" to. *Four Thousand Weeks* by Oliver Burkeman is a great read for gaining perspective on life and the way we approach the time we have for life, work, or play.[12]

Material Management

Controlling inventory is probably (hopefully) something your company already has in place. If not, or if you are an entrepreneur looking

---

[10] https://www.amazon.com/Big-Leap-Conquer-Hidden-Level/dp/0061735361/ref=tmm_pap_swatch_0?_encoding=UTF8&qid=1663259307&sr=8-1

[11] https://www.amazon.com/Secrets-Successful-People-Management-Straight/dp/0985056436/ref=tmm_pap_swatch_0?_encoding=UTF8&qid=1663259547&sr=8-1-spons

[12] https://www.amazon.com/gp/product/1784704008/ref=ewc_pr_img_2?smid=A3TJVJMBQL014A&psc=1

for the right tools, although I'm not endorsing any of these, here are some suggestions:

Oracle's NetSuite is considered one of the top systems, but it does much more than just inventory management and may not be what you are looking for. Or, it could cover all your needs as "a single, integrated suite of applications for managing accounting, order processing, inventory management, production, and supply chain and warehouse operations, NetSuite gives companies clear visibility of their data and control of their business."[13]

Fishbowl is more specifically designed to help manufacturing and warehousing companies. It includes: "inventory control, material requirements planning (MRP), job shop floor control, work order management, barcoding, raw materials management, manufacturer orders and bills of materials (BOM) and ability to predict inventory requirements based on sales trends."[14]

Point of Sale (POS) systems are another aspect of material management that are essential in all retail industries. Like inventory management systems, your company likely already has a POS system. If not, or if you are starting out with your own company, as owner/manager here are some systems that you might consider:

Block (formerly Square) is the original/modern small business solution for point of sale. The first Square systems plugged directly into smartphones; updated systems use Bluetooth or standalone hardware. Rated as the #1 POS system for 2022 by U.S. News and World Report, "Block offers POS systems geared toward retail stores, restaurants, and service businesses that work with customers by appointment, from home repair contractors to spas. It allows you to convert an iPhone,

---

[13] https://www.softwareadvice.com/inventory-management/netsuite-profile/
[14] https://www.softwareadvice.com/inventory-management/fishbowl-inventory-manufacturing -profile/

iPad, or Android device into a POS system by downloading its free Block POS app."[15]

If your company's presence is mostly or exclusively online, you might consider Shopify for your POS solution. Ranked #4 in U.S. News and World Report's 2022 rankings, Shopify offers a tiered system of services ranging in price (as of this printing) from $9 per month for the Lite service to $299 per month for the Advanced service.[16]

Like using barcodes to manage your inventory, radio-frequency identification (RFID) can keep track of everything you have on-hand in your store, warehouse, or distribution center. The advantage to using RFID over barcodes is that you don't need a line of sight between the item's tag and the reader. You can scan all items simply by being "in range" of your tags with the reading device. This will speed up the inventory process and by all rights, make it more accurate, and can be used to monitor. As this technology improves in quality and in popularity, the number of RFID options will no doubt grow too. While doing research for this book, I came across a review analysis site called "truely" which bills itself as "your lie detector for reviews." As with all things on the internet, you must decide for yourself if their claim is accurate, but their review of RFID systems can be found at https://truely.com/rfid-software.

Forecasting can be a very simple process using judgement and experience (qualitative methods), or it can be very detailed using data and regression analysis (quantitative methods). This makes forecasting a subject that could be its own book or course of instruction. If you want to dig deeper, a quick read and breakdown of the basics of forecasting can be found at https://www.universalclass.com/articles/business/the-art-and-science-of-forecasting-in-operations-management.htm.

---

[15] https://www.usnews.com/360-reviews/business/point-of-sale/block
[16] https://www.usnews.com/360-reviews/business/point-of-sale/shopify

Risk Management

Decisive, by Chip and Dan Heath,[17] is a great book on decision making. Worth noting, their discussion of a "pre-mortem" serves as one of the best explanations of how to do one and why it's important to reduce risk as well as make better decisions.

Doing something challenging with your team is a great way to get outside of comfort zones and to develop the habit of not getting complacent. Make sure your team is fit enough to do these events or find something else that everyone can do while still being challenged to leave their comfort zone. If there is a "zip line" or "ropes course" near you, they will have programs and experts who can guide you through team-building exercises.

For a team event, try Tough Mudder: https://toughmudder.com/
For individual events, try Spartan Race: https://www.spartan.com/

Change Management

A leader's intent statement is a great way to ensure your objective is achieved regardless of changes in the environment or the conditions you face. Here's an example of a leader's intent statement to keep your team on track and to allow them to use their initiative when things change:

Purpose: Improve the way new and reluctant managers take on their roles and balance how they manage regardless of condition.

Key Tasks:

1. **Publish** *Management in Balance*
2. **Market** book to clients and to industry leaders
3. **Speak** to managers via webinars, workshops, and lectures

---

[17] https://www.amazon.com/Decisive-How-Make-Better-Decisions/dp/1847940862/ref=tmm_pap_swatch_0?_encoding=UTF8&qid=1663276454&sr=1-1

End State: *Management in Balance* is a best seller, used by companies and individuals to improve their management skills, combined with *Leadership in Balance* to build stronger leaders.

Creating Network Diagrams can be a very complex task with lots of detail. Advances in computer software, artificial intelligence (AI), and machine learning (ML) are making this task easier to accomplish and more effective in understanding how individuals relate and communicate within groups and how groups interact with each other.

Palantir[18] is the gold standard for doing this across multiple disciplines and it was the preferred system used to see, understand, and act against insurgent and terrorist networks.

If you are interested in learning more about this and potential applications in a business environment (and you want to geek out), you might enjoy this thesis proposal from Tanzeem Khalid Choudhury at the Massachusetts Institute of Technology.[19]

---

[18] https://www.palantir.com/
[19] https://www.media.mit.edu/cogmac/prosem2007/tc_thesisproposal_may21.pdf

NOTES

Giving a Voice to Creativity!

With every donation, a voice will be given to the creativity that lies within the hearts of our children living with diverse challenges.

By making this difference, children that may not have been given the opportunity to have their Heart Heard will have the freedom to create beautiful works of art and musical creations.

Donate by visiting

HeartstobeHeard.com

We thank you.

Made in the USA
Columbia, SC
15 November 2022

71297370R00063